SPEAKING
Of
Success

INSIGHT PUBLISHING
SEVIERVILLE, TENNESSEE

SPEAKING
Of
Success

Published by Insight Publishing Company
P.O. Box 4189
Sevierville, Tennessee 37864

10 9 8 7 6 5 4 3 2

Printed in the United States of America

ISBN-13: 978-1-60013-146-2
ISBN-10: 1-60013-146-8

Table of Contents

A Message from the Publisher

When we decided to do a series of books on success, we searched long and hard to find just the right combination of authors who were not only a success in business but were successful in their personal life as well.

The authors we found had personal stories to tell that revealed their inner values—values that contributed to the achievements they have made and the positive influence they have on others. These authors are people whom others revere as persons of integrity. They are winners.

Everyone wants to be a winner. I have never met anyone who wants to be a loser. And I'm sure you haven't either. That's why we found some of the best motivational/inspirational speakers and authors in the country to contribute to this series. Some of these men and women are household names. Others are rising stars. All of them have achieved the kind of success all of us want—the kind that sparks enthusiasm in others and leaves an indelible, positive impression.

The road to success is one of hard work and persistence. *Speaking of Success* can help you unlock your potential and inspire you to realize the many possibilities awaiting you as you learn how to remove any mental blocks you might have to the success you deserve.

If you're already well on your way down the success highway, the stories and experiences of these authors will encourage you, inform you, and I guarantee that you will learn something.

It is with great pride that we Insight Publishing present this series, *Speaking of Success.* We think you will discover that you will find something new each time you read through these books.

The chapters in this series are real page-turners, so get ready to be inspired. Get ready to be delighted. Get ready to learn. And remember, *you* are the author of your own success journey. Others can shine a light on the path but you must do the walking.

Interviews conducted by:
David E. Wright
President, International Speakers Network

Chapter 1

MARSHA HAYGOOD

THE INTERVIEW

David Wright (Wright)

Marsha Haygood is President of StepWise Associates, LLC, a career and personal development consultancy whose mission is to offer professional and personal guidance to individuals and corporations through coaching, self-exploration, and motivational speaking.

Ms. Haygood founded StepWise to help individuals uncover and maximize their skills and talents. Through motivational speaking and personal coaching, she helps others realize their potential and fulfill their goals.

Marsha cultivated her coaching expertise during more than twenty-five years as an executive in Human Resources where she advised senior management and coached employees at all levels.

Ms. Haygood holds a Bachelor of Arts degree from Lehman College in New York and Human Resource Training and Development Certification from New York University. She is a member of the Society of Human Resource Management, New York Women in Film and Television, and the National Association of Female Executives. She has won numerous awards including the prestigious YMCA Black Achievement Award and the *Network Journal* magazine's Influential

Black Women in Business Award. She has also been featured in a number of publications for her contributions to corporate America.

Marsha, from your perspective, what would you say are some of the keys to success?

Marsha Haygood (Haygood)

First I believe that success means different things to different people. It is really a subjective term and the definition is somewhat personal. It's important to understand what it means to you personally so that you can work toward success on your terms and recognize opportunities for success when they present themselves.

For me it's not just about the salary earned or the title achieved, it means reaching my ultimate goal and doing the things that I enjoy and am passionate about. Starting my own business, helping others reach their potential, traveling, spending time with friends and family, and gardening all while having fun, is what success means for me personally.

Wright

You have had a successful career. What are some of the things that have helped you to achieve success?

Haygood

I believe that hard work is important, but working smart is equally important. By that I mean balancing work and personal life so that you don't burn out or miss important times with family. My husband and I both worked full-time while raising a family. He is really supportive of my career aspirations. My family truly wants me to succeed and just knowing that I have their support continues to build my confidence.

I also have some guiding principles that have helped me pave a path to success and fulfill my career and life goals. These include, first and foremost, developing an action plan and working toward fulfilling that plan and being flexible and open to opportunities. This has helped to prepare me for the next steps and has afforded me the opportunity to meet a diverse group of people and then cultivate those relationships.

I also believe that being prepared for change is critical. Since change is inevitable, I believe that preparing for it, expecting it, and being ready to embrace it rather than letting it overwhelm you is a key to success.

I believe it is also critical to remember that you shouldn't make excuses for things that do not go as you planned, but rather learn from your experiences—both the good and bad ones.

Wright

What lessons have you learned along the way that you would like to share with others?

Haygood

Oh boy, there have been many, and I can tell you that some I have learned the hard way. Some key lessons that I have learned include understanding that you must manage your career. I strongly believe that your career is an asset and should be managed as such. It is wise to make time to evaluate how you are doing and make adjustments along the way as needed. Chart the course you want to take but be flexible and open to opportunities that may come your way.

It's also important that you broaden your skills and your base of experience and go the extra mile. The key is to know something about a lot of things and learn about the business and industry you are in or that you want to be in, not just the job that you're currently doing.

I believe that it is also imperative that you learn to step outside your comfort zone and take prudent risks. To do so not only builds your confidence but allows you to tackle new challenges and helps you to grow.

I think that the hardest one for me to understand was that one is often more successful when everyone wins. What I mean is that you sometimes just have to leave something on the table so that everyone feels like they have gotten something out of the deal. There are some battles not worth fighting, even when you win, and others that must be fought, even if you lose. I guess the lesson is: pick your battles carefully.

Wright

Tell me more about your company, StepWise Associates.

Haygood

StepWise Associates is a business that I started in 2006 offering personal and professional guidance to those interested in working with a coach. Our mission is to help our clients develop strategies for personal and professional growth. We develop thought-provoking learning experiences through individual coaching, group facilitation, and motivational speaking engagements. We help both veteran and emerging leaders develop their goals and excel and succeed through self-exploration and planning. We establish a collaborative, supportive partnership with clients that allows them to discuss and further develop both life and career goals. We help clients assess their accomplishments and move forward based on these accomplishments and where they would like to be in the future.

Wright

You are a Career and Life Coach. Tell me more about what a Career and Life Coach does.

Haygood

The concept of coaching is simple and is becoming more popular in the business world today. A Career and Life Coach is similar to that of an Athletic Coach. We look at how you do things and help you develop your skills and tweak your techniques in order to reach a higher or different level. The best professionals in any given craft accept input, feedback, and criticism from their coach for continuous improvement. We help you build on your strengths and develop those areas you need to improve or do differently. A coach does not tell you what you must do but rather acts as your objective "thinking partner," helping you to create, plan, and implement strategies for your personal and professional growth.

Wright

How can coaching be used as a tool for success?

Haygood

Career and Life Coaching is a strategic development process and should really be used as such. We help our clients reflect on where they are currently and where they would like to be in the future. We then help them to develop a plan of action to get there. It's really building a vision and developing a personal plan of action. Often organizations hire a coach for an executive or emerging leader to help the individual round out his or her development. However, I believe that individuals should also invest in their own success and using a coach to help them in their development is a prudent and forward thinking way of doing that. A coach helps to provide perspective and clarity and can help you move forward personally and professionally.

Wright

As a coach, what advice do you give your clients regarding being successful?

Haygood

I tell my clients that they must first see themselves as successful and really believe that they can reach any goal they wish to attain. I then encourage and help them to develop an action plan. We work to set immediate, short-term, long-term, and ultimate goals and write them down. I strongly believe that goals give you something to work toward and writing them down gives you ownership.

I encourage clients to articulate their goals and let people know what they want to accomplish. Often people can help you if they understand what you are doing or seeking to accomplish. I also encourage them to solicit feedback and then be open to suggestions.

It's key, of course, to also form a good impression—always put your best foot forward and present a positive attitude; be mindful of the little details that make the difference.

I advise my clients to act and work outside the bounds of their job description and be willing to assume responsibility beyond their normal role. Sometimes they don't understand that, but I think its key. You can and should learn as much as possible about the things going on around you and do as much as possible to be a more well-rounded person. Be flexible and open to opportunities as they arise.

I think it's also important to understand that what you do for a living should not be the only way you define yourself. Work should not be your only focus. To be well-rounded you need to take time to enjoy life, to nurture yourself physically, mentally, and spiritually.

Wright

When a company hires a career coach for their prospective leaders, what control does the company have over the coaching process?

Haygood

The coaching process should be a collaborative one in that the company and the person being coached should know what to expect from the relationship and be able to articulate what outcome they would like to achieve.

To allow for an open, objective dialogue, it is imperative that all parties understand beforehand what information will or will not be shared. Once the intended outcome and the evaluation criteria are agreed upon, the coaching process can begin. The specifics of any assessments taken and conversations during the coaching sessions, by the company representative or by the client being coached are usually confidential.

Wright

What assurance does a company have that the person who is being coached will not leave for better opportunities once he or she has had a successful coaching experience?

Haygood

With the concept of employment at will, companies have no guarantee that employees will stay with them forever. However, employees are more likely to stay with a company that shows it values them, treats them fairly, and invests in their development. Hiring a coach is a good way for companies to show that they believe in employees' leadership ability and are willing to invest in their future. However, communication is also vital. Telling an employee that you value what he or she has to offer and planning out some of the areas you want the individual to develop in his or her career is important.

Wright

So if I were to hire a coach, what would you say are the attributes that I should look for?

Haygood

In my coaching relationships, I bring my experience in human resources, my experience as an entrepreneur, and my passion for working with and helping others to the process. A coach must also have good listening skills and be resourceful. However, I believe that it is integrity, trust, and developing a rapport that ultimately makes the coaching process work. I believe that these, as well as my collaborative coaching style, are all evident when I am working with clients and that these assets make for a successful relationship.

Wright

What are some of the obstacles people face in trying to become successful?

Haygood

That's a good question. I believe fear is a big obstacle in becoming successful. People say that they want success but then they are afraid to take prudent risks and step outside their comfort zone. I'm a strong believer that if you're too comfortable you're usually not growing.

Another obstacle is lack of preparation. Being prepared for opportunities when they arise (and they always do) is a key to success. I think you have to have your "elevator speech" ready. I think luck is one-half opportunity and the other half is preparation.

You also have to get the basics right. You have to perfect your craft, go the extra mile and practice, practice, practice. All too often, people want to rush to a bigger and better position without working on becoming better themselves.

Not learning from experiences can also be an obstacle. I believe that it is sometimes better to savor and learn from your experiences as well as the experiences of others. If you can learn from adversity as well as success then the obstacles are usually not so bad.

Wright

When you do workshops and speaking engagements, what are some of the issues you discuss?

Haygood

Depending on the audience, all of the topics mentioned previously are good workshop topics. However, goal-setting almost always comes up as a discussion point. I advise clients to think of goals as dreams with a deadline or a roadmap to a destination, and I encourage everyone I work with to put their goals in writing.

Other workshop topics include strategic networking, encouraging and accepting feedback, assessing your skills, confidence building, assessing your persona and style, transition preparation, marketing and branding yourself, and preparing for success to name a few.

Wright

What are some of the ways you would suggest preparing for success?

Haygood

The list is quite long and it continues to evolve but there are some success preparations that are definitely worth mentioning.

Once you decide what it is you want to do, you have to focus on it, be passionate about it, put positive energy toward it, and then practice, practice, practice.

You should learn from adversity and not dwell on mistakes but rather learn from them.

You should purge personal and professional relationships that drain your energy and then align yourself with people you want to learn from. Then put yourself in a position to be mentored.

You should build alliances and networking relationships.

And then last but not least, take time, at least annually, to re-evaluate where you are in terms of your goals and your life in general. Ask yourself: what is going well, what has worked thus far, what didn't work, and what is it that you would like to do differently?

I believe that everyone who wants to be successful is responsible for managing that process. People need to be strategic about their own self-development. Becoming successful is like running a business and that business is you!

Wright

What has been your proudest professional achievement to date?

Haygood

Wow, I feel that generally, my career has been a great accomplishment. I started as a part-time temp in a Human Resource department—at that time it was called Personnel—and moved through the ranks at various companies to Executive Vice President of Human Resources and Administration. In my last corporate position I oversaw Human Resources, Diversity, Facilities, Purchasing, Construction, and Travel in a major entertainment company. I'm proud of that. I'm also proud to have been featured in major publications for my work in corporate America. These have been great accomplishments for me and I have enjoyed these experiences. However, I think the best is still yet to come. I believe that my career continues to be a work in progress. There is still more to do and I am enjoying it to the fullest!

Wright

What a great conversation. I always love talking with successful people about success. You've given me a lot to think about here today and I really do appreciate your taking this time to answer these questions.

Haygood

David, it was very nice talking with you. I look forward to seeing the book in print.

About the Author

MARSHA HAYGOOD is President of StepWise Associates, LLC, a career and personal development consultancy whose mission is to offer professional and personal guidance to individuals and corporations through coaching, self-exploration, and motivational speaking.

Ms. Haygood founded StepWise to help individuals uncover and maximize their skills and talents. Through motivational speaking and personal coaching, she helps others realize their potential and fulfill their goals.

Marsha encourages you to think about where you are in life and where you would like to be. She inspires you to plan for your next steps both personally and professionally.

Marsha's coaching, workshops, and presentations center on personal awareness in order to help you make informed choices in alignment with your career and life goals. She helps clients discover their own greatness and move forward with purpose.

Ms. Haygood holds a Bachelor of Arts degree from Lehman College in New York and Human Resource Training and Development Certification from New York University. She is a member of the Society of Human Resource Management, New York Women in Film and Television, and the National Association of Female Executives. She has won numerous awards including the prestigious YMCA Black Achievement Award and the *Network Journal* magazine's Influential Black Women in Business Award. She has also been featured in a number of publications for her contributions to corporate America.

Marsha Haygood
StepWise Associates
One Glenwood Avenue – Lobby
Yonkers, NY 10701
Phone: 914.965.1339
E-mail: mhaygood@stepwiseassociates.com
www.stepwiseassociates.com

Chapter 2

DR. KEN BLANCHARD

David E. Wright (Wright)

Few people have created a positive impact on the day-to-day management of people and companies more than Dr. Kenneth Blanchard, who is known around the world simply as Ken, a prominent, gregarious, sought-after author, speaker, and business consultant. Ken is universally characterized by friends, colleagues, and clients as one of the most insightful, powerful, and compassionate men in business today. Ken's impact as a writer is far-reaching. His phenomenal best-selling book, *The One Minute Manager®*, co-authored with Spencer Johnson, has sold more than thirteen million copies worldwide and has been translated into more than twenty-five languages. Ken is Chairman and Chief Spiritual Officer of the Ken Blanchard Companies. The organization's focus is to energize organizations around the world with customized training in bottom line business strategies based on the simple, yet powerful principles inspired by Ken's best-selling books.

Dr. Blanchard, welcome to *Speaking of Success*!

Dr. Ken Blanchard (Blanchard)

Well, it's nice to talk to you, David. It's good to be here.

Wright

I must tell you that preparing for your interview took quite a bit more time than usual. The scope of your life's work and your business, the Ken Blanchard Companies, would make for a dozen fascinating interviews. Before we dive into the specifics of some of your projects and strategies, will you give our readers a brief synopsis of your life—how you came to be the Ken Blanchard we all know and respect?

Blanchard

Well, I'll tell you, David, I think life is what you do when you are planning on doing something else. I think that was John Lennon's line. I never intended to do what I have been doing. In fact, all my professors in college told me that I couldn't write. I wanted to do college work, which I did, and they said, "You had better be an administrator." So I decided I was going to be a Dean of Students. I got provisionally accepted into my master's degree program and then provisionally accepted at Cornell, because I never could take any of those standardized tests.

I took the college boards four times and finally got 502 in English. I don't have a test-taking mind. I ended up in a university in Athens, Ohio, in 1966 as an Administrative Assistant to the Dean of the Business School. When I got there he said, "Ken, I want you to teach a course. I want all my deans to teach." I had never thought about teaching because they said I couldn't write, and teachers had to publish. He put me in the manager's department.

I've taken enough bad courses in my day and I wasn't going to teach one. I really prepared and had a wonderful time with the students. I was chosen as one of the top ten teachers on the campus coming out of the chute!

I just had a marvelous time. A colleague by the name of Paul Hersey was chairman of the management department. He wasn't very friendly to me initially because the Dean had led me into his department, but I heard he was a great teacher. He taught organizational behavior and leadership. So I said, "Can I sit in on your course next semester?"

"Nobody audits my courses," he said. "If you want to take it for credit, you're welcome."

I couldn't believe it. I had a doctoral degree and he wanted me to take his course for credit, so I signed up.

The registrar didn't know what to do with me because I already had a doctorate, but I wrote the papers and took the course, and it was great.

In June 1967, Hersey came into my office and said, "Ken, I've been teaching in this field for ten years. I think I'm better than anybody, but I can't write. I'm a nervous wreck, and I'd love to write a textbook with somebody. Would you write one with me?"

I said, "We ought to be a great team. You can't write and I'm not supposed to be able to, so let's do it!"

Thus began this great career of writing and teaching. We wrote a textbook called *Management of Organizational Behavior: Utilizing Human Resources*. It came out in its eighth edition October 3, 2000 and the nineth edition will be out June 15, 2007. It has sold more than any other textbook in that area over the years. It's been over forty years since that book came out.

I quit my administrative job, became a professor, and ended up working my way up the ranks. I got a sabbatical leave and went to California for one year twenty-five years ago. I ended up meeting Spencer Johnson at a cocktail party. He wrote children's books—a wonderful series called *Value Tales for Kids including.* He also wrote *The Value of Courage: The Story of Jackie Robinson* and *The Value of Believing In Yourself: The Story Louis Pasteur.*

My wife, Margie, met him first and said, "You guys ought to write a children's book for managers because they won't read anything else." That was my introduction to Spencer. So, *The One Minute Manager* was really a kid's book for big people. That is a long way from saying that my career was well planned.

Wright

Ken, what and/or who were your early influences in the areas of business, leadership and success? In other words, who shaped you in your early years?

Blanchard

My father had a great impact on me. He was retired as an admiral in the Navy and had a wonderful philosophy. I remember when I was elected as president of the seventh grade, and I came home all pumped up. My father said, "Son, it's great that you're the president of the seventh grade, but now that you have that leadership position, don't ever use it." He said, "Great leaders are followed because people respect them and like them, not because they have power." That was a wonderful lesson for me early on. He was just a great model for me. I got a lot from him.

Then I had this wonderful opportunity in the mid 1980s to write a book with Norman Vincent Peale. He wrote *The Power of Positive Thinking*. I met him when he was eighty-six years old and we were asked to write a book on ethics together, *The Power of Ethical Management: Integrity Pays, You Don't Have to Cheat to Win*. It didn't matter what we were writing together, I learned so much from him, and he just built from the positive things I learned from my mother.

My mother said that when I was born I laughed before I cried, I danced before I walked, and I smiled before I frowned. So that, as well as Norman Vincent Peale, really impacted me as I focused on what I could do to train leaders. How do you make them positive? How do you make them realize that it's not about them, it's about who they are serving. It's not about their position, it's about what they can do to help other people win.

So, I'd say my mother and father, then Norman Vincent Peale, all had a tremendous impact on me.

Wright

I can imagine. I read a summary of your undergraduate and graduate degrees. I assumed you studied business administration, marketing management, and related courses. Instead, at Cornell you studied government and philosophy. You received your master's from Colgate in sociology and counseling and your PhD from Cornell in educational administration and leadership. Why did you choose this course of study? How has it affected your writing and consulting?

Blanchard

Well, again, it wasn't really well planned out. I originally went to Colgate to get a master's degree in education because I was going to be a Dean of Students over men. I had been a government major, and I was a government major because it was the best department at Cornell in the Liberal Arts School. It was exciting. We would study what the people were doing at the league governments. And then, the Philosophy Department was great. I just loved the philosophical arguments. I wasn't a great student in terms of getting grades, but I'm a total learner. I would sit there and listen, and I would really soak it in.

When I went over to Colgate and got in these education courses, they were awful. They were boring. The second week, I was sitting at the bar at the Colgate Inn saying, "I can't believe I've been here two years for this." It's just the way the Lord works—sitting next to me in the bar was a young sociology professor who had just gotten his PhD at Illinois. He was staying at the Inn. I was moaning and groaning about what I was doing, and he said, "Why don't you come and major with me in sociology? It's really exciting."

"I can do that?" I asked.

He said, "Yes."

I knew they would probably let me do whatever I wanted the first week. Suddenly, I switched out of education and went with Warren Ramshaw. He had a tremendous impact on me. He retired some years ago as the leading professor at Colgate in the Arts and Sciences, and got me interested in leadership and organizations. That's why I got a master's in sociology.

The reason I went into educational administration and leadership? It was a doctoral program I could get into because I knew the guy heading up the program. He said, "The greatest thing about Cornell is that you will be in a School of Education. It's not very big, so you don't have to take many education courses, and you can take stuff all over the place."

There was a marvelous man by the name of Don McCarty, who eventually became the Dean of the School of Education, Wisconsin. He had an impact on my life; but I was always just searching around. My mission statement is: to be a loving teacher and example of simple truths that help myself and others to awaken the presence of God in our lives. The reason I mention "God" is that I believe the biggest addiction in the world is the human ego; but I'm really into simple truth. I used to tell people I was trying to get the B.S. out of the behavioral sciences.

Wright

I can't help but think, when you mentioned your father, that he just bottomed lined it for you about leadership.

Blanchard

Yes.

Wright

A man named Paul Myers, in Texas, years and years ago when I went to a conference down there, said, "David, if you think you're a leader and you look around, and no one is following you, you're just out for a walk."

Blanchard

Well, you'd get a kick; I'm just reaching over to pick up a picture of Paul Myers on my desk. He's a good friend, and he's a part of our Center for FaithWalk Leadership where we're trying to challenge and equip people to lead like Jesus. It's non-profit. I tell people I'm not an evangelist because we've got enough trouble with the Christians we have. We don't need any more new ones. But, this is a picture of Paul on top of a mountain. Then there's another picture below that of him under the sea with stingrays. It says, "Attitude is everything. Whether you're on the top of the mountain or the bottom of the sea, true happiness is achieved by accepting God's promises, and by having a biblically positive frame of mind. Your attitude is everything." Isn't that something?

Wright

He's a fine, fine man. He helped me tremendously. In keeping with the theme of our book, *Speaking of Success,* I wanted to get a sense from you about your own success journey. Many people know you best from *The One Minute Manager* books you coauthored with Spencer Johnson. Would you consider these books as a high water mark for you, or have you defined success for yourself in different terms?

Blanchard

Well, you know, *The One Minute Manager* was an absurdly successful book, so quickly that I found I couldn't take credit for it. That was when I really got on my own spiritual journey and started to try to find out what the real meaning of life and success was.

That's been a wonderful journey for me because I think, David, the problem with most people is they think their self-worth is a function of their performance plus the opinion of others. The minute you think that is what your self-worth is, every day your self-worth is up for grabs because your performance is going to fluctuate on a day-to-day basis. People are fickle. Their opinions are going to go up and down. You need to ground your self-worth in the unconditional love that

God has ready for us, and that really grew out of the unbelievable success of *The One Minute Manager.*

When I started to realize where all that came from, that's how I got involved in this ministry that I mentioned. Paul Myers is a part of it. As I started to read the Bible, I realized that everything I've ever written about, or taught, Jesus did. You know, He did it with the twelve incompetent guys He "hired." The only guy with much education was Judas, and he was His only turnover problem.

Wright

Right.

Blanchard

It was a really interesting thing. What I see in people is not only do they think their self-worth is a function of their performance plus the opinion of others, but they measure their success on the amount of accumulation of wealth, on recognition, power, and status. I think those are nice success items. There's nothing wrong with those, as long as you don't define your life by that.

What I think you need to focus on rather than success is what Bob Buford, in his book *Halftime,* calls significance—moving from success to significance. I think the opposite of accumulation of wealth is generosity.

I wrote a book called *The Generosity Factor* with Truett Cathy, who is the founder of Chick-fil-A. He is one of the most generous men I've ever met in my life. I thought we needed to have a model of generosity. It's not only your treasure, but it's your time and talent. Truett and I added *touch* as a fourth one.

The opposite of recognition is service. I think you become an adult when you realize you're here to serve rather than to be served.

Finally, the opposite of power and status is loving relationships. Take Mother Teresa as an example; she couldn't have cared less about recognition, power, and status because she was focused on generosity, service, and loving relationships; but she got all of that earthly stuff. If you focus on the earthly, such as money, recognition, and power, you're never going to get to significance. But if you focus on significance, you'll be amazed at how much success can come your way.

Wright

I spoke with Truett Cathy recently and was impressed by what a down-to-earth, good man he seems to be. When you start talking about him closing on Sunday, all of my friends—when they found out I had talked to him—said, "Boy, he must be a great Christian man, but he's rich and all this." I told them, "Well, to put his faith into perspective, by closing on Sunday it cost him $500 million a year."

He lives his faith, doesn't he?

Blanchard

Absolutely, but he still outsells everybody else.

Wright

That's right.

Blanchard

According to their January 25, 2007, press release, Chick-fil-A is currently the nation's second-largest quick-service chicken restaurant chain in sales. Its business performance marks the thirty-ninth consecutive year the chain has enjoyed a system-wide sales gain—a streak the company has sustained since opening its first chain restaurant in 1967.

Wright

The simplest market scheme, I told him, tripped me up. I walked by his first Chick-fil-A I had ever seen, and some girl came out with chicken stuck on toothpicks and handed me one; I just grabbed it and ate it, it's history from there on.

Blanchard

Yes, I think so. It's really special. It is so important that people understand generosity, service, and loving relationships because too many people are running around like a bunch of peacocks. You even see pastors who measure their success by how many in are in their congregation; authors by how many books they have sold; business-people by what their profit margin is—how good sales are. The reality is that's all well and good, but I think what you need to focus on is the other. I think if business did that more and we got Wall Street off our backs with all the short-term evaluation, we'd be a lot better off.

Wright

Absolutely. There seems to be a clear theme that winds through many of your books that have to do with success in business and organizations—how people are treated by management and how they feel about their value to a company. Is this an accurate observation? If so, can you elaborate on it?

Blanchard

Yes, it's a very accurate observation. See, I think the profit is the applause you get for taking care of your customers and creating a motivating environment for your people. Very often people think that business is only about the bottom line. But no, that happens to be the result of creating raving fan customers, which I've described with Sheldon Bowles in our book, *Raving Fans*. Customers want to brag about you, if you create an environment where people can be gung-ho and committed. You've got to take care of your customers and your people, and then your cash register is going to go ka-ching, and you can make some big bucks.

Wright

I noticed that your professional title with the Ken Blanchard Companies is somewhat unique—Chairman and Chief Spiritual Officer. What does your title mean to you personally and to your company? How does it affect the books you choose to write?

Blanchard

I remember having lunch with Max DuPree one time, the legendary Chairman of Herman Miller, who wrote a wonderful book called *Leadership Is An Art*. "What's your job?" I asked him.

He said, "I basically work in the vision area."

"Well, what do you do?" I asked.

"I'm like a third grade teacher," he replied. "I say our vision and values over, and over, and over again until people get it right, right, right."

I decided from that, I was going to become the Chief Spiritual Officer, which means I would be working in the vision, values, and energy part of our business. I ended up leaving a morning message every day for everybody in our company. We have twenty-eight international offices around the world. I leave a voice mail every morning, and I do three things on that as Chief Spiritual Officer: One, people tell me who we need to pray for. Two, people tell me who we need to praise—

our unsung heroes and people like that. And then three, I leave an inspirational morning message. I really am the cheerleader—the Energizer Bunny—in our company. I'm the reminder of why we're here and what we're trying to do.

We think that our business in the Ken Blanchard Companies is to help people lead at a higher level, and to help individuals and organizations. Our mission statement is to unleash the power and potential of people and organizations for the common good. So if we are going to do that, we've really got to believe in that.

I'm working on getting more Chief Spiritual Officers around the country. I think it's a great title and we should get more of them.

Wright

So those people for whom you pray, where do you get the names?

Blanchard

The people in the company tell me who needs help, whether it's a spouse who is sick, or kids who are sick, or they are worried about something. We've got over five years of data about the power of prayer, which is pretty important.

One morning, my inspirational message was about my wife and five members of our company who walked sixty miles one weekend—twenty miles a day for three days—to raise money for breast cancer research.

It was amazing. I went down and waved them all in as they came. They had a ceremony, and they had raised 7.6 million dollars. There were over three thousand people walking, and a lot of the walkers were dressed in pink; they were cancer victors—people who had overcome it. There were even men walking with pictures of their wives who had died from breast cancer. I thought it was incredible.

There wasn't one mention about it in the major San Diego papers. I said, "Isn't that just something." We have to be an island of positive influence because all you see in the paper today is about Michael Jackson and Scott Peterson and Kobe Bryant—celebrities and their bad behavior—and here you get all these thousands of people out there walking and trying to make a difference, and nobody thinks it's news.

So every morning I pump people up about what life's about, about what's going on. That's what my Chief Spiritual Officer job is about.

Wright

I had the pleasure of reading one of your releases, *The Leadership Pill.*

Blanchard

Yes.

Wright

I must admit that my first thought was how short the book was. I wondered if I was going to get my money's worth, which by the way, I most certainly did. Many of your books are brief and based on a fictitious story. Most business books in the market today are hundreds of pages in length and are read almost like a textbook.

Will you talk a little bit about why you write these short books, and about the premise of *The Leadership Pill?*

Blanchard

I really developed my relationship with Spencer Johnson when we wrote *The One Minute Manager.* As you know, he wrote, *Who Moved My Cheese*, which was a phenomenal success. He wrote children's books, and is quite a storyteller.

Jesus taught by parables, which were short stories.

My favorite books are, *Jonathan Livingston Seagull* and *The Little Prince.*

Og Mandino, author of seventeen books, was the greatest of them all.

I started writing parables because people can get into the story and learn the contents of the story, and they don't bring their judgmental hats into reading. You write a regular book and they'll say, "Well, where did you get the research?" They get into that judgmental side. Our books get them emotionally involved and they learn.

The Leadership Pill is a fun story about a pharmaceutical company who thinks that they have discovered the secret to leadership, and they can put the ingredients in a pill. When they announce it, the country goes crazy because everybody knows we need more effective leaders. When they release it, it outsells Viagra. The founders of the company start selling off stock and they call them Pillionaires. But along comes this guy who calls himself "the effective manager," and he challenges them to a no-pill challenge. If they identify two non-performing groups, he'll take on one and let somebody on the pill take another one, and he guarantees he will out-perform that person by the end of the year. They agree, but of course they give him a drug test every week to make sure he's not sneaking pills on the side.

I wrote the book with Marc Muchnick, who is a young guy in his early thirties. We did a major study of what this interesting "Y" generation, the young people of today, want from leaders, and this is a secret blend that this effective manager uses. When you think about it, David, it is really powerful on terms of what people want from a leader.

Number one, they want integrity. A lot of people have talked about that in the past, but these young people will walk if they see people say one thing and do another. A lot of us walk to the bathroom and out into the halls to talk about it. But these people will quit. They don't want somebody to say something and not do it.

The second thing they want is a partnership relationship. They hate superior/subordinate. I mean, what awful terms those are. You know, the "head" of the department and the hired "hands"—you don't even give them a head. "What do you do? I'm in supervision. I see things a lot clearer than these stupid idiots." They want to be treated as partners; if they can get a financial partnership, great. If they can't, they really want a minimum of psychological partnership where they can bring their brains to work and make decisions.

Then finally, they want affirmation. They not only want to be caught doing things right, but they want to be affirmed for who they are. They want to be known as a person, not as a number.

So those are the three ingredients that this effective manager uses. They are wonderful values when you think about them.

Rank-order values for any organization is number one, integrity. In our company we call it ethics. It is our number one value. The number two value is partnership. In our company we call it relationships. Number three is affirmation—being affirmed as a human being. I think that ties into relationships, too. They are wonderful values that can drive behavior in a great way.

Wright

I believe most people in today's business culture would agree that success in business has everything to do with successful leadership. In *The Leadership Pill*, you present a simple but profound premise, that leadership is not something you do to people, it's something you do *with* them. At face value, that seems incredibly obvious. But you must have found in your research and observations that leaders in today's culture do not get this. Would you speak to that issue?

Blanchard

Yes. I think what often happens in this is the human ego. There are too many leaders out there who are self-serving. They're not leaders who have service in mind. They think the sheep are there for the benefit of the shepherd. All the power, money, fame, and recognition moves up the hierarchy; they forget that the real action in business is not up the hierarchy; it's in the one-to-one, moment-to-moment interactions that your front line people have with your customers. It's how the phone is answered. It's how problems are dealt with and those kinds of things. If you don't think that you're doing leadership *with* them—rather, you're doing it to them—after a while they won't take care of your customers.

I was at a store once (not Nordstrom's, where I normally would go) and I thought of something I had to share with my wife, Margie. I asked the guy behind the counter in Men's Wear, "May I use your phone?"

He said, "No!"

"You're kidding me," I said. "I can always use the phone at Nordstrom's."

"Look, buddy," he said, "they won't let *me* use the phone here. Why should I let you use the phone?"

That is an example of leadership that's done *to* employees not *with* them. People want a partnership. People want to be involved in a way that really makes a difference.

Wright

Dr. Blanchard, the time has flown by and there are so many more questions I'd like to ask you. In closing, would you mind sharing with our readers some thoughts on success? If you were mentoring a small group of men and women, and one of their central goals was to become successful, what kind of advice would you give them?

Blanchard

Well, I would first of all say, "What are you focused on?" If you are focused on success as being, as I said earlier, accumulation of money, recognition, power, or status, I think you've got the wrong target. What you need to really be focused on is how you can be generous in the use of your time and your talent and your treasure and touch. How can you serve people rather than be served? How can you develop caring, loving relationships with people? My sense is if you will focus on those things, success in the traditional sense will come to you. But if you go out and say, "Man, I'm going to make a fortune, and I'm going to do this," and have that kind of attitude, you might get some of those numbers. I think you become an adult, however, when you realize you are here to give rather than to get. You're here to serve not to be served. I would just say to people, "Life is such a very special occasion. Don't miss it by aiming at a target that bypasses other people, because we're really here to serve each other." So that's what I would share with people.

Wright

Well, what an enlightening conversation, Dr. Blanchard. I really want you to know how much I appreciate all the time you've taken with me for this interview. I know that our readers will learn from this, and I really appreciate your being with us today.

Blanchard

Well, thank you so much, David. I really enjoyed my time with you. You've asked some great questions that made me think, and I hope my answers are helpful to other people because as I say, life is a special occasion.

Wright

Today we have been talking with Dr. Ken Blanchard. He is the author of the phenomenal best selling book, *The One Minute Manager*. The fact that he's the Chief Spiritual Officer of his company should make us all think about how we are leading our companies and leading our families and leading anything, whether it is in church or civic organizations. I know I will.

Thank you so much, Dr. Blanchard, for being with us today on *Speaking of Success*.

Blanchard

Good to be with you, David.

About The Author

Few people have created more of a positive impact on the day-to-day management of people and companies than Dr. Kenneth Blanchard, who is known around the world simply as "Ken."

When Ken speaks, he speaks from the heart with warmth and humor. His unique gift is to speak to an audience and communicate with each individual as if they were alone and talking one-on-one. He is a polished storyteller with a knack for making the seemingly complex easy to understand.

Ken has been a guest on a number of national television programs, including *Good Morning America* and *The Today Show*. He has been featured in *Time, People, U.S. News & World Report*, and a host of other popular publications.

He earned his bachelor's degree in government and philosophy from Cornell University, his master's degree in sociology and counseling from Colgate University, and his PhD in educational administration and leadership from Cornell University.

Dr. Ken Blanchard
The Ken Blanchard Companies
125 State Place
Escondido, California 92029
Phone: 800.728.6000
Fax: 760.489.8407
www.kenblanchard.com

Chapter 3

KAREN FRIEDMAN

David Wright (Wright)

Today we're talking with Karen Friedman. She is one of the leading communications coaches in today's business world whose techniques are successfully used by thousands of people across the globe. Founder of Philadelphia-based Karen Friedman Enterprises, Inc., she counsels spokespeople, newsmakers, and executives to make the most of every interview, appearance, meeting, and presentation. Karen's expertise in message development was first recognized when a U.S. delegation led by former First Lady Hillary Rodham Clinton tapped her to provide media and political training for women in South and Central America. She continues to counsel clients worldwide. A member of the National Speakers Association who has repeatedly received the International Association of Business Communicators top-rated speaker designation, she is frequently quoted by top tier publications including the *New York Times* and *Wall Street Journal.*

Karen, welcome to *Speaking of Success.*

When people ask you what it takes to be successful, what do you tell them?

Karen Friedman (Friedman)

Never stop dreaming! No matter how old you are or what curveballs life throws you, you have to visualize your own success. And you should never stop believing in yourself. I also tell people what my parents told me and what I tell my own children: you can do anything you want to do if you want it badly enough. Granted, if you're not mathematically inclined, you probably won't succeed as a nuclear physicist—but it's not always about how smart you are, it's about how badly you want something.

I remember staring out my dormitory window in college and picturing myself as a major market television newscaster earning a great living. And after college, when I left Philadelphia and moved to Alabama to become a television reporter, people thought I was nuts. So many people told me it wasn't realistic—that there are thousands of people who wanted to be on television and only a few spots in the top markets. I can't even begin to tell you how many people told me I wouldn't succeed.

What you learn is that you can't let other people's negativity interfere with your dreams and how you see yourself. You have to taste it. It's like preparing for an important speech. I tell my clients to close their eyes, see the audience hanging onto their words, see them clapping, smiling, see them learning. You need to feel it.

Success means different things to different people. To some it's money, to others it's fame, and to others it's about giving and helping. Success is personal and only you can define what it means to you.

Wright

In your opinion, what characteristics do you think sets successful people apart from those who are not successful?

Friedman

From my vantage point as a communicator, it is someone's ability to communicate clearly, passionately, and personally. It's so important to take the time to understand what a listener cares about so you can communicate one-on-one regardless of whether you are talking to one person or one thousand people. Think about great communicators like Oprah, Bill Clinton, Ronald Reagan, Abraham Lincoln, Martin Luther King—these people have taken complicated concepts and explained them in bite-sized nuggets that are relevant and meaningful to listeners.

In my own business, I work with a lot of doctors, technology whizzes, scientists, and healthcare executives. Quite frankly a lot of these people are much smarter than I am. But often what they say is just beyond what most of us can comprehend. Successful people engage and motivate by understanding what an audience or employee or boss cares about, so what they say is important to that person. When you learn to do this, people care about what you have to say. If they care because it affects them, then they feel. If they feel, they listen.

I'll give you an example. A number of years ago, I ran for a seat in the Pennsylvania State House and my opponent was a lawyer who was on the state's Land Planning Commission and helped write the municipal code. At the time, the big issue was sprawl, which was good for her because she knew a lot about it. It wasn't so good for me because I didn't know much about it. Every time we were both interviewed on the issue, she was quoted and I wasn't.

Then all of a sudden, it hit me. People didn't really care about sprawl. They cared about how sprawl affected them. They cared about traffic, pollution, open space being gobbled up, and dangers to their children. So, the next time I was asked about it, I said, "Traffic is so bad out here in Montgomery County that I could balance my checkbook on the way home from work." My quote made it into *Business Week*, and from then on every time I was interviewed, I kept saying the same thing. I kept getting quoted and my opponent, far more of an expert than I was, did not.

Wright

You just mentioned that you ran for a seat in the Pennsylvania State House—I understand that you lost in absentee votes. What did that failure teach you that you can share with our readers?

Friedman

It reminded me that there is no such thing as failure. Going back to what I said, you can't let someone else define you with their choice of words or beliefs. It's like riding a bike. You have to fall off a lot of times before you can stay on the seat. In business as in life, every time we lose our footing on a ladder and slip a step, we should treat it as a gift because we're being given an opportunity to learn, to grow, and to do it better the next time. Think of businesses that have weathered crises and have became stronger than ever because they asked the right questions: How can I do it better? What actions can I take to right the wrong? How would I react if I were in someone else's shoes? I think that's the key. You have to sit in your listeners' seats and become them. As a coach, I clearly understood that, but running for office actually made me better at helping other people see it. As a candidate, I knocked on 25,000 doors and listened to people's concerns. These people just wanted to be heard, even if you couldn't fix their problems.

That's where former Secretary of Defense Donald Rumsfeld missed an opportunity in 2006 when he suggested that the American people had unmistakably rejected how the Iraq war was being handled because they were not wise and knowledgeable enough to understand it. That's like calling someone stupid. Regardless of your political stance, every one of us wants to be heard—to feel that what we say matters. Being a candidate constantly reminded me that when I spoke, it wasn't about me. It's been my mantra to my clients ever since.

Wright

How did your first career as a television news reporter and anchor prepare you to coach executives?

Friedman

Television reporters have this unique ability to think on their feet and dumb down even the most complicated concept. We had this little newsroom joke when we weren't given enough time for a story or we perceived that management thought promoting the story was more important than the story itself. We would say: *Don't let the facts get in the way of a good story.* In television, what that really means is grab people's attention and then sustain it with great sound bites, pictures, and gut-wrenching stories if you want people to tune in. Executives are afraid that if they get away from biz speak and speak simply, people won't take them seriously—that they won't be perceived as smart or credible—so they use big words and industry jargon and keep talking to make themselves sound smart when in fact the opposite is true. Instead of connecting, captivating, and making their message really easy to understand and remember, they confuse listeners and quite frankly end up being pretty boring.

Executives can learn some very simple lessons from television reporters: (1) Get to the point, (2) Put yourself in your listeners' shoes so you can address what they really want to know instead of focusing on everything you think you need to tell them, and (3) Keep it Simple.

Wright

How do women create their own obstacles and what advice can you give them?

Friedman

My biggest piece of advice to women is to stop trying to act like men. We're *not* men, and I believe that is our strength. Of course it is important to be treated equally and given the same opportunities. We should be forever indebted to the women before us who fought for our rights, bucked convention, and spawned the women's movement. But, it is equally important to tap into our inner strengths as women and to use those to our advantage wherever and whenever possible.

For example, women are nurturing, soft, outspoken, and tend to wear their emotions on their sleeve. While we need to be careful not to over-react and create confrontation, the same qualities that people tell us to subdue are actually warm, endearing, and often make us more approachable than many men. So, if you are a female CEO or if you manage employees, you may be able to use these skills to build loyalty and get more from people, including your customers.

I remember working as a reporter at ABC television in Philadelphia when my oldest son was two years old. As I was leaving for work, the pre-school called to tell me he was sick and I needed to pick him up. My husband was out of town and I had no one to stay with him. I had to get to work, so I called the station and explained it to my female boss who said, we're already down two reporters and while I'm sorry your son is sick, that really isn't our problem and you have to come to work. I was dumbfounded and obviously pretty upset. As I was about to hang up, she said to me, "Listen, call back in about five minutes, but when you ask for me, don't mention your problem. Just tell me you're sick and can't get out of bed." That's exactly what I did. A male boss may have been compassionate, but I'm not sure he would have given me the same nurturing advice.

Wright

What is the best advice you can give to people who are already successful and want to stay at the top of their game?

Friedman

Stay real and always imagine possibilities! Remember what you longed for before you had any clout or money and before anyone knew who you were. Someone you were nasty to on your way up the ladder might be in a position to affect your future one day. It's so important to treat everyone with the same respect. Don't kiss up to the board members and treat the mailroom clerk like a peon. Most of us learn this the hard way and some of us never learn it at all.

When I was a television reporter, there were always on-air people who thought they were more important than the story they covered. These are the same people who sucked up to management, but treated camera crews and production people like second class citizens. What they failed to realize is those production people could make them look good or bad and also make or break their careers.

Wright

You've been called one of the leading communication coaches in today's business world. What strategies do you teach that make the biggest difference for others?

Friedman

People tell me I help them think differently and see things differently. I think I make them feel safe because I give them permission to make mistakes—to let people know they're human so people can relate to them. And I constantly remind them that they are the expert, which is why audiences or reporters have come to them to hear what they have to say.

Then I tell them what my dad told me. Joe Friedman always said: "If you look good, you feel good. If you feel good, you do good." So, that's the starting point. Come to every interview, meeting, presentation, or public appearance with your game face on. Every time you speak, it's a performance. It's the Super Bowl, and who knows when you'll get this chance again? Roger Ailes, CEO of Fox News, wrote a great book called *You Are the Message.* So you need to make sure, as he says, that your tone, attitude, attire, and body language are as strong as what you have to say, and that all of you reflects your message.

I work with a lot of really bright people who have to share ideas at meetings on a regular basis. Because they are experts in their field, they sometimes forget that not everyone knows what they know and as a result they miss huge opportunities to gain buy-in or move their agenda forward. They come to these meetings with cluttered slideshows that they stand and read to the audience. They don't realize that putting together slides is not communicating. I tell people before they write or create a slideshow or a presentation to think about the take-home—the one thing they want people to remember in three days or three weeks or three months—to really focus on the message so the slides follow them instead of the other way around.

And finally, I tell them that no matter how glib they are to *never wing it.* Even the most seasoned communicator consults a road map. The map, or organizational model, that we build in our coaching sessions will get you from point A to B to Z so your message is focused, organized, crisp, clear, and appeals on a very personal level. And that is what is so significant—learning how to drive your message home with real life examples, anecdotes, vignettes, visual images, or powerful data because that's what people remember. We'd like to think that if we deliver a compelling argument or motivational talk, people will hang on to our every word. Well, they might hang for the moment if we're lucky, but they won't remember most of what we said. They'll remember stories and they'll remember how we made them feel.

Wright

You quit a successful career as an on-air newscaster at ABC in Philadelphia, which was and still is the number one local television station in the country. You built a six-figure coaching practice. What lessons can you share with others?

Friedman

Fear is a great motivator. We're scared of failing, ruining our reputations, embarrassing ourselves, and I think the more successful we are, the more fearful we are that somehow it's going to all go away. I've been in business for more than a decade but I still have days where I fear the phone won't ring or that I won't make a difference in somebody's life. But that keeps me going.

When I left a twenty-year career in television, in all honesty I was terrified. What did I know about business? What skills did I have that would benefit others if I wasn't writing stories for television newscasts? Where would I get clients? And once I had them, what would I do with them? But then I asked myself: what's the worst that can happen? I could fail. Okay, so if I fail, so what? If I didn't make it, I could always go get a "real" job.

In my case, I left my career in television when I felt like I was stagnating—I was starting to cover the same stories over and over and I was no longer growing personally or professionally. From the bottom of my heart I believe it's important to take risks in order to grow. In my own case I lost sleep for three years trying to figure out what I wanted to do next and what I wanted to be when I grew up.

But not making any decision at all is far worse and far more frustrating than making a bad one. I think you have to make decisions and see them through, but you shouldn't make them in a vacuum—do your homework, consult your colleagues and trusted advisors, and have a plan. If it doesn't work and the door closes, another door will always open. That's what makes life so interesting. We simply don't know what's around the corner.

Wright

In recent years, so many well known celebrities and newsmakers like Michael Richards (Kramer from *Seinfeld*), Mel Gibson, and Donald Rumsfeld have been in the news for making mistakes. Some, like Martha Stewart, have even gone to jail. As someone who has navigated many companies and spokespeople through crises, can we learn lessons from their mistakes that we can apply to our own lives and careers?

Friedman

Absolutely. First we have to realize that we live in a very different world than our parents or the generations before us. In this age of blogs, Web sites and chat rooms, there is no such thing as privacy. What you do, say or e-mail can and will come back to haunt you in a much bigger way than ever before.

Take Michael Richards for example, best known as the hilarious Cosmo Kramer in *Seinfeld*. People loved him and as many of us know he lost it and started screaming racial slurs at hecklers during a performance in Hollywood. And here's what is unfortunate—no matter how fabulous he was—a brilliant comedian and actor—he'll be remembered as this guy who ranted and made slurs. Every time a story is written about him, someone will mention that tirade, which will overshadow his brilliant successful career.

There are so many lessons to learn from other people's blunders, but most importantly, don't make excuses. Own up to what you did or what you said and apologize; but only do so if that apology is heartfelt and sincere. Don't expect people to forgive just because you said you're sorry or you check into rehab. You have to earn back that trust and respect and help others realize why you did what you did. Help them learn from your mistakes.

Wright

To whom do you attribute your own drive and successful career? Who were your mentors?

Friedman

My parents are my mentors and have always been my biggest cheerleaders. From as early as I can remember, I was encouraged to follow my dreams and to listen to my heart. My father's passion is music. He is a wonderful piano player, but he went into the family business because his parents didn't encourage or support his creative dreams. They didn't help him believe in himself and his ability to do what he loved. They didn't encourage him to follow his heart and I believe it is his single greatest regret.

Like my dad, my mother strongly encouraged me to chase my dreams, to be independent, happy, and not to follow the crowd. She is the epitome of optimism and beamed at the simplest accomplishments of my two brothers and me, always bragging and believing in our ability to do anything. I remember hearing her gush to her friends when I was a kid and I always had such a warm glow inside—she created such self-esteem in all three of us. She has always been my rock.

So if not for my mother and my father, I don't know if I would have believed in myself and I don't think I would be as confident and as able to pick myself up every time I fell down without their support and encouragement.

Wright

You are married with two children. How do you balance family and career?

Friedman

I wish I had a magic bullet to answer that one for you, but I don't. It is difficult. There is never enough time in the day and like many parents, I always feel guilty. If I am traveling and working hard, I feel a bit neglectful of my family. If I am having too much fun, I feel as if I'm not working hard enough. I just try my best and I try not to beat myself up too much.

For example, I was traveling last week and had a lot of catch-up work to do in my office on Sunday. But I also had not spent time with my children. The work will always be there, but as my children get older, I realize more now than ever that it's only a matter of time until they aren't home anymore. I spent the day with them; we went to the movies and grabbed a bite to eat, and I just tried to be in the moment instead of worrying about what was waiting for me back in my office.

You have to constantly remind yourself to be present, to enjoy the little moments, and remind yourself what's really important.

Wright

What are the best pieces of advice you can offer to others who want to be successful?

Friedman

First, never stop believing in yourself. When someone doubts you or tells you that you can't do something, let that energize and motivate you to try harder to reach your goals.

Don't compare yourself to others. There will always be someone smarter, richer, and prettier. Be yourself and realize that you will be more successful when you make others successful. So, empower and help those around you to reach their full potential if you want to reach yours.

Never stop learning, growing, or striving to re-invent yourself. Read everything you can get your hands on and be open to other viewpoints even if you don't agree.

Look for opportunities to travel or interact and get to know people from different cultures. You will learn tolerance and you will realize that despite cultural, philosophical, and religious differences, we are similar in so many ways.

And remember, your definition of success will constantly change as you change. Embrace that change and define your own definition of success and what it means to you.

Finally, if you're twenty, thirty, fifty, or ninety, never stop dreaming and always follow your heart!

Wright

What a great conversation. It's been such a pleasure asking you all these questions. You've given me some of the greatest answers, and I'm going to think about these things!

About the Author

KAREN FRIEDMAN is one of the leading communication coaches in today's business world. An award-winning television news anchor and reporter whose breaking coverage of local and national events aired on ABC, CBS, NBC, CNN, the *Today Show, Good Morning America,* and *Nightline,* she now teaches executives, spokespeople, and newsmakers across the globe how to make the most of every interview, appearance, meeting, and presentation. Karen's expertise in message development was first recognized when a U.S. delegation led by former First Lady Hillary Rodham Clinton tapped her to provide media and political training for women in South and Central America. She continues to counsel key opinion leaders worldwide.

For more than a decade, spokespeople have been relying on Karen's know-how to develop and deliver meaningful messages during nationwide awareness campaigns, manufacturing shutdowns, Justice Department inquiries, product launches, investor and community meetings, employee presentations, chemical spills, government hearings, and the drug approval process. She taught journalism at the University of Wisconsin and once ran for a hotly contested seat in the Pennsylvania State House.

Frequently quoted by top-tier publications such as the *New York Times, Wall Street Journal,* and *Harvard Business Review,* Karen is a professional speaker who has repeatedly received the International Association of Business Communicators top-rated speaker award. She resides in the Philadelphia area with her wonderful husband, two incredible sons, a neurotic dog, and ornery cat.

Karen Friedman
Karen Friedman Enterprises, Inc.
P.O. Box 224
Blue Bell, PA 19422
Phone: 610.292.9780
E-mail: Karen@KarenFriedman.com
www.KarenFriedman.com

Chapter 4

MICHAEL MAYER

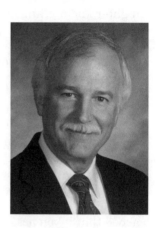

THE INTERVIEW

David Wright (Wright)

Michael Mayer is a licensed psychologist, consultant, and author of four books who has a driving passion to help others personally succeed in their various roles as leaders, professionals, partners, parents, and with themselves. "We need to take responsibility for the way we touch those lives around us yet we generally only know one way—our way." By looking at our personal traits and challenging their effectiveness, we become better leaders of others and ourselves.

Dr. Mayer helps those in business and in professions better reach their level of expertise through the following ways:

1. He works with individuals to help them get to their next level of personal growth and success.
2. He works with teams to develop better and more productive working relationships.
3. He works leading retreats, training, and personalized group problem-solving.

4. He works in intense and confidential one-on-one focus meetings.

He has worked with individuals, businesses, and professional groups, including professional offices, hospitals, family businesses, religious groups, and state offices. He has authored four books, he has a live radio program, he has written articles for magazines, and presented at state and national meetings. He is married and has a daughter and a granddaughter. He loves the challenge of making others good motivators and leaders.

Michael, do you know what makes a person successful as a leader and if so, how do you know this?

Michael Mayer (Mayer)

That's a question I usually ask leaders: "What makes you think you are a good leader?" Leaders must know their roots. Unfortunately we don't pay much attention to how our roots affect us as leaders and thus affect those we lead.

Let me give you some things to think about regarding how your roots might affect you as a leader: Did you learn as a child growing up that to lead you must be more powerful than others? Maybe you learned that if you act as though you know what you are doing others will follow you regardless of your abilities. You may have been taught that what others think or feel doesn't matter—what you say goes because you are the person in authority. Possibly you were taught that understanding and cooperating with others can make you a great leader.

It does matter what you've learned early in life about leadership and what you learned does affect your style of leading others today. Go back and examine your family of origin's influence on your leadership skills. Maybe some of your parents were smarter than you thought or maybe what you learned was incorrect.

Wright

Who taught you how to be a leader?

Mayer

I'm glad you asked that question. Everyone should have a mentor. My father was a wonderful human being who taught me how to lead. I also learned from the people who had leadership roles in my life and also from the people I've had as clients. Clients can teach a lot about leading if we listen to them with an open mind.

There is so much more to learn about people than we already know. There is so much more to learn about our influences on those we lead.

Wright

What are seven inter-related qualities of an effective leader?

Mayer

I've put them in an acronym that as you go along spells out GET REAL. "GET REAL," is not the slang expression used today. What I mean by GET REAL is that as a leader you need to be a real person in order to be an effective leader. Let's look at each of these qualities:

1. *Good listener.* Unfortunately most of us are very poor listeners. We over-estimate our ability to listen. I find that to be true in most businesses and in most personal relationships. We have to be able to accurately understand and repeat back what we've heard from others. That sounds very simple but it is difficult to do because we don't take time to do that and we assume people understand what we are telling them. Haven't you heard from your significant other that you "never listen" to him or her?

2. *Expectations* of performance are clear for self and others. (I will touch upon this later.)

3. *Trusted* by those who follow you. Getting those you lead to trust you will be a constant but worthwhile challenge. People you lead want you to tell the truth and not abuse your power. Trust does not come easy.

4. *Rules and boundaries* are justly established. Everyone needs guidelines. We forget that if there are no guidelines people might not naturally follow what needs to be done. They need someone to give them some guidelines. Most complaints in business come from employees not knowing what is expected of them. Keep your rules and boundaries fair.

5. *Explicit purpose and vision* for all those you lead. If you don't have a purpose they won't have a purpose. They need to buy into your purpose as a leader and they need to feel a part of that purpose.

6. *Attitude* as a motivator is positive and passionate. How often have you heard that? Have passion. You look for the positive qualities in others and convey strong feelings about what you do and what you want them to do. You do not want to be a boring "preacher."

7. *Looking* out for others, not just taking care of yourself—in other words "other focused." This ties in closely with attitude.

If you want to be an effective leader, these seven qualities are important for you to remember to effectively be able to help others reach their next level of productivity.

Wright

Do the people you lead really understand what is expected of them and then have you provided them time, place, and materials needed to accomplish this task?

Mayer

Unfortunately, what I have seen happen in people trying to understand what a leader expects is not very often accomplished. There is a book I like to quote when I talk about employer expectations and it's called, *First Break All the Rules,* by Marcus Buckingham and Kurt Kauffman. They studied 80,000 mangers and over a million employees. Some of the most important findings they discovered were some questions that people need answers for to be satisfied with work.

Two of the most important questions that employees came up with were: Do I know what is expected of me at work? Do I have the materials and equipment I need to do my work right? These questions show why it's important as a leader for you to be able to clearly delineate what is expected of those who work for you. Provide the materials they need and give them the time and the place in order to accomplish that task. Many people, unfortunately, have not made a priority of learning what is expected of them on the job.

More importantly, it is possible that the owner or the leader doesn't truly understand what tasks or skills the job really requires and ends up hiring someone who can't do the job. Maybe the expectations are not achievable by anyone. This also needs to be examined.

My advice is that you need to clearly outline the task required by the job using the help of others who have worked in that position or who have observed what others have done in that particular job. Write these tasks in words that can be understood by the average employee. That's very important because as you cross train you should not have a problem. Make those job expectations clear enough to the potential employee so that he or she can explain to you what is required to meet your expectations.

When the minds, words, expectations, and purpose meet between you and the employee you will have a winning situation.

Wright

Can you get out of who you are enough to help others reach their potential?

Mayer

That is a tough thing to do because we like ourselves a little too much. Leadership is not a "what is in it for me" situation. I think we can learn to focus on others and that's what we are looking for in leadership. Constant self-focused behavior doesn't cut it in the leadership roll. Make positive comments about what others are accomplishing; that's a must. People operate better with praise than criticism. Leaders need to make positive comments to employees daily.

My experience in the workplace and in other settings has proven to me that finding and encouraging others' strengths produces better people and therefore better employees. Often without thinking about it people follow leaders' examples every day and if leaders are primarily critical in their approach to managing, then employees will tend to be critical of their leaders, co-workers, and the place where they work. They will leave when the opportunity arises because who wants to work in a negative environment? Good leaders know how to change an employee's behavior by being direct and to the point but avoiding personal and non-effective criticism.

All people feel better and do better when you give them your time and truly appreciate their efforts. So your goal is to find employees' strengths and use these strengths to make them productive. When you add to a person's life he or she reacts better to you as a leader. When you take away from employees' lives they withdraw and turn from you and your messages. If you can't say something constructive to a person, then a least have the decency to be vague.

Wright

Are questions or answers more important in being a leader?

Mayer

Definitely questions are more important and I will give some examples of questions in just a moment. You know so little about those you lead and you can't lead them without understanding how they think and operate within their system and how they react to your system.

Asking questions about how they operate in their world gives you the needed information to make them successful employees, partners, and individuals. Several questions to ask employees come immediately to mind: Can you tell me in your words what you understand to be the demands of your job? What strengths do you posses to meet the job as we have explained it to you? How can we help you achieve your goals in working here? Is there anything you would like us to know about you? Do you have any concerns about our expectations of you? What in your opinion makes a workplace a place where you want to work?

I think these are a few of the important questions you might ask as you get to know your employees. It is easy to tell others what to do but do we have the skills to ask the right questions to get the information we need?

Wright

Change is necessary for growth as a leader. What are you as a leader planning to change?

Mayer

As a leader I think we all need to be willing to make changes in order to grow. We know so little about how to lead, but all indicators point to understanding those we lead as critical to our growth as leaders. If fear blocks those we lead, we need to know what it takes to move them beyond their fear and into action.

If you're not aware of what you as a leader need to change to facilitate your personal growth, it might help you to ask trusted friends or significant others in your life what they see as your strengths and weaknesses. Use this information to help you decide your next area of personal growth.

Every day that we experience life and its events we are changed in some way. Being aware of how life effects us and how it changes the way we affect others is vital information needed for a leader to continue his or her effectiveness. We often forget that we as leaders project onto others our thoughts, feelings, and personal beliefs. We need to claim and understand this and determine whether it is valuable and equitable. We need to know what in our personal system keeps us from helping those we lead from attaining their purpose in the workplace. We need to know what our passion is as a leader and whether we communicate this effectively to those we lead.

Do you know where you are going as a leader? Do you understand the next step you need to take to achieve that goal? Are you willing to change? If not, you could lose some of your effectiveness as a leader.

Wright

What are the reasons people follow a leader?

Mayer

That's an interesting question. As a leader, have you ever asked yourself that question and then thought, "I have no idea"? Hopefully the answer is that they follow you as a leader because they believe in you and because you believe in them—not because of your belief about yourself as a leader. Leadership is not about you, it is about your helping others do their best to attain the goal they cherish.

More people want to follow than lead so it is your responsibility to treat those you lead with care. Their lives are under your influence. Do you have the values and vision needed to lead these people?

Wright

Where do people need the influence of a good leader?

Mayer

Basically everywhere. I know that's easy to say but we all need to lead and be led at some point in our lives. We can be a leader to our children, share leadership with our spouses, lead others to spiritual growth, and lead others to success in the workplace. We all have some person—adult or child—who looks up to us for answers or direction.

There are other places in life where a larger group may ask you to lead them. The workplace setting comes to mind first. Here's a place where you can have a great impact on others. To do so you must have mind, body, emotions, and spirit intact. Family, marriages, and friends can fall into the category of needing a leader, but may involve a different set of skills. Remember, you are the same leader who needs to learn appropriate adaptations to each setting using the leadership skills mentioned earlier. Be a leader in life and learn to follow when appropriate.

Wright

On the top of your list of seven qualities you started with—being a good listener—I recently heard one man say that in today's world people don't communicate, they just take turns talking. I don't know if that is true or not.

Mayer

That is true. For example, when you were talking to me I heard what you said but I was also preparing my answer. What often happens in preparing your answer is that you could miss something someone is saying to you. Your mind is distracted with preparing your defense or your answer. Most people do get diverted while another person is talking.

One of the other problems in listening is that we hear what others say and hear it from our perspective.

I have a program on radio and I love it. I present a life concern and then give solutions. One of the things I like to remind listeners is that when you listen to others you don't truly understand the meaning of their words unless you were born in their family, have their genetics, and have all their learning experiences. These elements make up their frame of reference. When they talk to you, they hear you from their frame of reference. Now you can begin to realize that you'd better start asking what others mean by what they say rather than assume you know the answer.

"Get the job done well" is a great example of not knowing what is expected. The message is not clear. Doing something well varies from person to person. "I love you" can mean so many things to so many people. Only you know what love means to you. You need to know a person very well before you will understand what love means to him or her.

A true listener will be a very successful person and a good leader. If you truly master listening, you will be a better leader.

Wright

A question about another item in the seven important qualities of effective leaders is number five—explicit purpose and vision for all those you lead. How does a leader develop an explicit purpose and vision for those people they lead? Since the people in various settings are different, would that purpose and vision be different?

Mayer

This statement applies to a lot of different settings. I'm going to limit my discussion to the workplace setting because that's where most people are leaders. There are some general purposes you want to try to explain to employees. A purpose at work may be that we want to put "service to our customers" as a number one priority.

The vision is a little more global and purposes are a little more specific. The vision will be more general such as, "Where are we going?" and, "What are we trying to accomplish?" These are sometimes called Mission Statements.

The explicit purpose, on the other hand, would be trying to explain to people why you are here, why you are at this workplace, and what your purpose is for working here. You can make your own purposes that you've gleaned from talking to other people within the business. Start with your own purposes for the workplace and then update them as you grow as a business and as you gather more people with new ideas. I also like people to answer the question, "What's your purpose in life?" Then narrow it down to, "What's your purpose for working for this particular leader or employer?"

Your employees also have to have their own purpose along with the purpose their leader is proposing to them. Hopefully these purposes mesh because when they do, you have a better match within the workplace.

Wright

What should readers take away with them from reading this chapter and how will they implement that knowledge?

Mayer

I think it's very important that you realize you are a leader and to be successful you must understand yourself first. (I discussed this in the beginning of the chapter.) Then understand those you lead.

To understand yourself you may have to go talk with people you know or maybe talk to a professional. There's a lot of coaching currently available. I also enjoy coaching others, especially executives. The purpose of this coaching is to help them understand how they interact with others, how they've been influenced by all of their experiences in their life, and how these experiences have affected them as a leader and as someone who's giving advice to others.

Then you need to understand those you lead. To understand those you lead you need to start some type of a program to find out more about the people who work for you. The bigger the company, the less you're going to know everyone. Someone needs to know the people within that workplace.

There are people who have made the effort and taken the time to know the people within their business. Salespeople keep notes on people they want to try to influence so that when they call on them as prospective clients they can relate to them on a personal level. They can ask about an individual client's son or daughter or they can talk to clients about a favorite hobby or sport. What is important about this is that you show you are interested enough in the other person to remember facts about each of your clients' lives. If you are in a leadership position it is important to know employees' strengths and weaknesses. If you don't know that information, then a manager who works directly with employees should know because it is important for the business to capitalize on each employee's strengths. You want to let employees know that they are a part of the entire team. They then can look up to their leaders not only because they've taken time and energy to try to allow them to use their strengths but their leaders have also helped them feel that they are individuals as well as employees. You have been given the privilege to lead others, use it wisely.

Wright

What a great conversation. I really appreciate your answers to these questions. I appreciate the time that you've taken to enlighten me and our readers. I really appreciate it.

Mayer

Thank you, David. Maybe I should end with one last statement. Leadership style is changing. GET REAL, the concept put forward in that acronym, will help you transform into the most effective leader possible.

Wright

Today we have been talking with Dr. Michael Mayer who is a licensed psychologist, consultant, and the author of four books. Dr. Mayer helps those in business better reach their level of expertise. He works with individuals to get to the next level of growth and success. He works with teams to develop better productive working relationships. He leads retreats, training, and personalized group problem-solving. He also works confidentially in one-on-one focus meetings.

Dr. Mayer, we really appreciate your participating in this project. We're so glad that you've been with us today on *Speaking of Success.*

Mayer

Thank you very much David.

About the Author

MICHAEL MAYER has been actively involved helping business leaders, professionals, and individual business owners find more effective and productive ways to organize and manage the "people side" of business. Mike has helped professionals and executives through difficult phases of their personal and professional lives using one-on-one problem and person-focused meetings. He loves to speak at conventions, training seminars, and conduct retreats. He is also available for radio and television programs. Over the past few years he has influenced many with his live radio programs. Three of the four books he has authored are currently available. He loves to be challenged by difficult situations involving people and workplaces.

Michael Mayer
Mayer, Flanagan, Scott, and Associates
3407 Berrywood Drive, Suite 200
Columbia, MO 65201
Phone: 573.443.1177
E-mail: mmayer1019@aol.com
www.mikemayer.com

Chapter 5

JAMES ROSWELL QUINN

THE INTERVIEW

David Wright (Wright)

James Roswell Quinn is an international keynote speaker, success coach, and leadership trainer. Since 1979, he has made nearly 1,400 presentations to over 150,000 people worldwide. James has spoken to organizations such as Walt Disney Feature Animation, Microtel, and the Nightingale-Conant Corporation.

Quinn has authored the self-help book, *Controlling Others for Love and Profit,* and recorded the eight-CD personal audio seminar, "Get Over Yourself."

James, welcome to *Speaking of Success.*

James Roswell Quinn (Quinn)

It's a pleasure to be here David.

Wright

So, how do you define "success," and how do people objectively measure their results from using your tools and concepts?

Quinn

As I see it, success is the ability to create desired results, and that differs for everybody.

Years ago, I attended a conference where Earl Nightingale was speaking. During his talk, he shared his definition of success. Thinking it was brilliant, I wrote it down: *"Success is the active pursuit of a worthwhile goal."*

At first, I just loved that definition. However, after a while it felt like something was missing. Eventually I figured it out—it lacked a "results" component. It is not just the pursuit of a worthwhile goal, it is the creation of the desired result.

Sure, loving what you are doing is a wonderful thing for inner peace, but eventually you must create desired results. For example, managers do not want salespeople who try hard; they want people who make sales. Your bank is not interested in how sincerely you want to make this month's house payment; they want to see the check on time.

There is always an excuse for failure. Did you ever see anyone standing on a street corner shouting, *"Hey, I'm a self-made failure!"*?

Instead, we say things like, *"What do you expect from somebody who was raised by parents like mine?"* or *"I wouldn't be yelling at you if you weren't yelling at me"* or *"My boss never listens to me"* or *"The clients only care about price."* Even if we admit our mistakes, there is always somebody to blame.

When we make excuses, we can easily justify our non-productive and even destructive behaviors. When this happens, we become our own worst enemy, thus preventing our own success.

Successful people are those who are willing to change their own behavior after each failure. They know that somehow, they must do something differently to create desired results.

Fortunately, humans are the only beings on this planet that can consciously change their own behaviors. Unfortunately, the normal reaction to change is resistance. Hence, most people make excuses instead of changing.

There will always be issues and problems, but you will not always have desired results—not unless you are willing to do whatever it takes to create those results. Success, therefore, is the combination of knowing what your desired results are, and then doing whatever it takes to create them. Intentions equal results, is not just a theory. It's the bottom line.

Success does not just happen. You have to create it. My successful students follow this simple formula:

Step One: **Define Exactly What You Want.** You must be clear and specific regarding your desired results.

Step Two: **Enjoy The Process.** Earl Nightingale was right: *"Success is the active pursuit of a worthwhile goal."*

Step Three: **Change Your Self.** The negative circumstances that "trigger" your non-productive or self-destructive behaviors are not the problem. The problem is, your negative reactions were "trigger-able." You need to be aware enough to see it, and then change your behavior rather than try to control or change other people.

Wright

What is the single most important ingredient needed for people to create success?

Quinn

I've given that a lot of thought. We've kicked it around in seminars all over the world. I have come to the conclusion that there is not just one, but four ingredients that are needed to create success.

To me the first ingredient has to be *Determination.* Some may say it is education, product knowledge, or luck, but people make their own luck—and the world is full of educated derelicts. It seems to me that determination is a key element to creating desired results.

My family and I live in a rural area. There's a restaurant/bar near our home, with a sign above the entrance that reads, *"Get 'er Done"* (which I think was there before Larry the Cable Guy trademarked the phrase). I love that sentiment. If you intend to create desired results, then you must have the determination to do whatever it takes.

First, we have to be aware of what we are doing. Then, if it isn't creating desired results, we need to make adjustments. Therefore, we need to pay attention to what does and what does not work.

In my leadership seminars, there are two jobs and one rule:

Job One: **Get The Job Done.** If you have a vision and have the integrity to make a commitment to that vision, you must have the determination to get the job done.

Job Two: **Identify Your Obstacles.** By identifying the problems and issues that are in your way, or that could get into your way, you dramatically increase the odds of getting the job done.

The Rule: Never Let *Job Two* Take Priority Over *Job One.* I find that people who do not look for what might go wrong find themselves unprepared for, and then beaten by unforeseen circumstances. The opposite approach is even worse. People who are consumed by their problems and obstacles tend to avoid taking any action at all.

Tools such as positive thinking, worst-case scenario planning, and belief in philosophies such as "The Law of Attraction" can help us, but only if we put something into action. We can fail and we can lose. We may fail again and lose again, but eventually there must be a victory.

Determination, however, is not to be confused with stubbornness. Albert Einstein observed, *"The definition of insanity is doing the same thing over and over again and expecting different results."* If you never give up on your quest for desired results, and learn from each failure, then you must succeed.

Hoping for success does not create your desired results. My father used to say, *"Hope is just a ship that travels around picking up dead bodies."* Determination, not hope, creates success.

The truth is, anything that can stop you will stop you. To have the determination to create a desired result is to know that if you fall, you will get back up. If you fail, you will learn from the failure and do something different the next time.

Nothing can stop you if you have faith in your vision and faith in yourself. To be determined is to know that nothing will stop you. You are not going to quit until you get the job done. This is where success comes from.

Wright

So, what's the second ingredient?

Quinn

The second ingredient is *Balance.* In fact, balance is the key to "sustaining" success.

As much as we all want to think that having a lot of money will make us happy, success cannot be defined by wealth alone. If money solved our problems, the Betty Ford Clinic would not have so many rich, famous, and powerful patients. There is more to success than money, fame, or power.

Many "successful" people have ended their lives as failures. John Belushi overdosed on drugs at the height of his career. Kurt Cobain killed himself and he had millions of dollars in the bank. Ken Lay, the powerful CEO and chairman of the Enron Corporation, died a convicted felon. When successful people cannot sustain their success, it's always because their lives lack balance.

Balance is key. To create and sustain success, we need physical health, emotionally supportive relationships, a stimulating career, and a spiritual connection. We need to balance it all.

Murphy's Law states that if something can go wrong, it will go wrong. Without balance all the monetary success in the world will not create happiness and fulfillment. What value does money have without good health, a higher purpose (a spiritual component), and people with whom you can share your success (an emotional component)?

Balance is key. When I am coaching clients on business issues, the main goal is not to get them to be successful at their careers. When coaching clients wishing to improve a relationship, the main goal is not to improve the relationship. In either case, my focus is getting people to bring themselves into balance.

If you are ignoring your health, you are going to pay the price. If you are ignoring your business, you are going to pay the price. If you are ignoring your wife, husband, or life partner, you are going to pay the price. If you are living a life without a higher purpose, in your final days you will feel hollow and empty because your life will seem meaningless.

Someone once said, *"If you don't change where you're going, you're going to end up where you're heading"*—even if you do not see it coming. The more focused you are on one part of your life, the greater the likelihood that you will miss the warning signs of a problem developing in another.

I coach people toward a "4 x 4 Effect." You achieve a "4 x 4 Effect" when you focus your efforts to create desired results in all four major areas of life: Physical, Emotional, Mental, and Spiritual. Balanced efforts create balanced results. Balanced results give you something to lean on when there is an issue or problem in one area.

Balance keeps you on your path during those times when the world seems to pull the rug out from underneath you. Interestingly, by making you pay attention, your problems are actually helping you to create balance.

Success requires balanced results. When I coach clients, their health and energy increases, their relationships become more fun and loving, they make more money working fewer hours, and they go to bed with a heightened sense of fulfillment and peace. Balance is key.

Wright

And the third ingredient of Success?

Quinn

Celebration. To my father, celebration was practically everything. He was my mentor and my coach. He taught me not only to celebrate my successes, but to celebrate my failures. Celebrate. Celebrate. Celebrate. The phrase I recall him using the most often was, *"The only thing more contagious than enthusiasm, is the lack of it."* Celebrate everything.

Are you celebrating your life? If you are on the phone with clients, are you sitting or standing? Are you showered and shaved and dressed for success? Do you keep a mirror near the phone so you can see if your expression is joyful? If they could see you, would they be inspired? If you were shopping for a car, would you be motivated by a salesperson who is reclining in a chair, at a messy desk, unshaven, grubby, and frowning? Celebrate everything. Enjoy shining your shoes.

Edison is a wonderful example of celebration. He made thousands of unsuccessful experiments to develop the light bulb—thousands. I can imagine trying something and failing eight or nine times. I might be able to stretch it to 100 or 200, but 9,999 failures (or whatever the exact amount was) is beyond my comprehension.

At first glance, Edison's determination is evident. However, this determination was fueled by his ability to celebrate. He celebrated his failures by learning something from each of them. To Edison, a failed experiment was not wrong because it failed—it was a lesson. That is what he celebrated.

Most of us are willing to attempt to make a relationship or a job work, but rarely change our approach by learning from each failure. We just move from job to job or relationship to relationship, but end up doing the same thing over and over again without celebrating the lessons—without learning, without changing, and without succeeding.

Edison used the knowledge gained in each failed attempt to invent the light bulb as his path to finally achieve his desired result—*light!* If he had merely repeated the original experiment 10,000 times without changing something, he would have been committed to a rest home. He celebrated his failures as lessons learned by tracking them to eventually determine what would work.

Most people resist changing, even if what they are doing is not working. It's time to recognize that resistance to change is the root of the problem.

For us to celebrate life, we need to recognize, *"People are a lot like fruit. When they're green they grow, and when they're ripe they rot."* (This statement by Bernard Baruch, an elder U.S. statesman, became the motto for McDonald's CEO, Ray Kroc.)

We need to celebrate the process of growing because our actions always produce something—either the desired result or a lesson. If you only celebrate your successes, and you are negative about your failures, you will have fewer successes.

Wright

This brings us to the fourth ingredient of success, which is?

Quinn

Empathy. People are surprised when I say that; but empathy—the ability to feel what others feel or are going to feel—is a key to success.

Long before he became a successful businessman and a politician, one of my mentors was told the secret to success was, *"Other people have everything you want. To be successful, find out what they want and what motivates them and then make sure they get what they want first."* In other words, do not focus on what you are going to get, focus on what you are going to give.

Mother Teresa put it even stronger. She said, *"It is not what you do, it is how much love you put in the doing. And it is not what you give, it is how much love you put in the giving."* As the proverb says, *"Givers gain and takers lose."*

With empathy, there is energy in giving. And we can teach it to others. For example, when a child comes to you and says, *"Can I help you make your bed?"* let the child do just that. And if they mess it up, don't admonish or correct them. Instead, take pictures of the rumpled bed and slap the picture on the fridge, with a sign that says, *"My kid helped me do this today!"* Start inspiring people to become givers.

I love it when people say things like, *"I'm exhausted. I've tried everything and I can't get my spouse to listen to me"* or *"I'm so exhausted. I've tried everything and my prospects won't buy"* or *"I'm exhausted. I've tried everything and my boss won't change"* or *"I can't get other people to do what I want, I'm exhausted!"*

I ask, *"You've been giving it everything you've got?"* When they say, *"Yes,"* then I ask, *"And you're exhausted?"* They always respond,

"Yes." I find that answer to be interesting. So I ask you, *"Is giving exhausting?"*

Let's look at a real-life example. Have you ever shopped for a gift and become frustrated because you couldn't find what you wanted? Then, suddenly, you turn down an aisle and there it is. You think, *"Oh my God. I can't believe it. She [or he] is just going to love this!"*

When you got home, you wrapped the present with special paper, ribbon, and extra tape. Maybe you used a box within a box, within a box, within a box. You were energized and filled with joy just thinking about the moment it would be opened. Then, on the big day, you handed the person this special gift and said, *"I couldn't resist getting this for you."* When the person opened it, his or her breath stopped. *"Where did you find this?"* the person might have asked with eyes lit up as he or she gave you that special look.

Was that exhausting? Of course not—true giving is energizing. When coming from empathy, *"The gift is in the giving."* Even if you also received gifts that day, you probably felt more joy during this moment.

However, when you lack empathy and come from judgment, fear, expectation, or disappointment, you are not energized. Without empathy, regardless of what you do or what you give, I question that you are actually giving.

When you lack the empathy to walk in another person's shoes, you do something in order to get something back. Resentment invariably results, and you will use that fact to justify your own resistance to the other person. You will stop giving with joy. This is exhausting.

Behold the magnificent apple tree. It never says, *"I only give my apples to the deserving."* An apple tree that stops bearing fruit, regardless of the reason, is exhausted—it is, in fact, dying.

Just as apple trees, humans are natural beings. We too are not immune from the laws of nature. When you and I stop giving, whether it's because we are frustrated, hurt, worried, angry, tired, or resentful—whatever the reason—we too are exhausted. We too are dying.

Having empathy empowers us to be better givers. We see the value in others and want them to see ours. We need to have empathy for the people we disagree with or whom we don't understand.

We need empathy to discover what other people's needs are and then to fill those needs. Only then do we have a chance for success.

Wright

You keep mentioning your father. What did he teach you about success?

Quinn

During his speaking career, my father taught nearly 2,400 of his LifeStream personal growth seminars to over 200,000 people. While most of these four-, five- and six-day programs were taught in the United States and Canada, he also conducted several in New Zealand and Israel.

Wherever he taught, people were moved to change their lives. I can still hear his voice, *"Your life works in direct proportion to the commitments you make and keep."*

I could write an entire book on what I have learned from him. However, if I had to narrow it down, the most valuable thing I learned from James Holden Quinn was the importance of listening to my heart. *"Trust yourself, Ross,"* he would say. *"You've got a great mind, you've got a fast mind, and you can do anything you want with your life."* He often said to me, *"Follow your dreams."*

Unfortunately, most people do not follow their dreams. Instead, they react to their circumstances. They are happy when treated with honor and respect, and miserable when mistreated or ignored. They are not motivated by the creation of their desired results but, rather, by the prevention of their negative results.

The main reason most people do not have what they want is they are too busy trying to prevent getting what they don't want. What motivates you, creating wealth or preventing poverty? Are you striving to create a loving relationship or are you more focused on preventing it from ending?

When tempted to react negatively, ask yourself, *"What do I really want? Am I creating what I want or am I trying to prevent getting what I don't want?"*

Edison was a visionary. He did not create the light bulb by trying to prevent darkness. He had a desired result and did what it took to make it manifest.

The same is true for you and for me. We cannot create success by trying to prevent failure. A visionary is someone whose desired results are more important than the problems and issues they face.

Since there are few visionaries, I coined the word "Victim-ary," to describe everyone who isn't one. A victimary is someone whose issues and problems override their desired results. Typical victimary statements include, *"I'm only yelling at you because you're yelling at me,"* or *"I'm quitting because they never listen to me"* or *"If I tell you what I need, you might disappoint me again"* or *"If I tell you the truth, you'll probably use it against me"* or *"I don't get mad, I get even."*

Victimaries justify behaviors they know to be ineffective when used by others. These negative reactions do not create long-term desired results.

Any justified behavior that keeps you from creating your desired results is a problem. Instead of putting the focus on "why" you are reacting negatively, put your focus on "how" you are reacting. Then, by overcoming the negativity that other people have triggered, you automatically increase your chances for success.

My father taught me to be myself. He often said, *"We are human beings, not human doings."* His message was, *"Be who you are."*

The challenge is, you can't be who you are if you don't know who you are. When you know who you are, you can no longer be defined by emotional states such as, *"I am mad," "I am sad," "I am nervous"* or negative circumstances such as, *"I am unemployed," "I am late," "I am broke," "I am a failure,"* and so on.

There will always be issues and problems. There will always be reasons to react negatively. My father taught me the value of choosing to overcome my negative reactions. He taught me to be myself.

Wright

Who else has inspired your success?

Quinn

My mother was, and continues to be, a major influence on my life. Janet Eve (Quinn) Sanders taught me about empathy and purpose. From her example, I learned to respect the feelings and attitudes of other people and to live my life with a higher purpose—a higher purpose than just taking care of myself.

My wife, Christine, has been a huge inspiration for my success. Her attitude is so positive. I heard my daughter emulating my wife on the phone the other day. She was advising her friend, *"Don't get caught up in negativity, be positive. Don't worry about him; you'll get another boyfriend. When he finally figures out he wants you, you'll have found somebody better."*

Christine passed her wisdom about the importance of a positive attitude to my children and me. Whenever one of the kids would say something negative, she would have them stand in front of a mirror and say the positive reversal of their negative statement three times. For example, if Shanairra said, *"I feel stupid,"* Christine would have her say out loud, *"I am smart, I am smart, I am smart."*

The kids would pretend to hate the process, but they would laugh and do it anyway. They also pretended to hate giving hugs, but they would do it. That kind of positive human interaction is essential.

I have learned "QuinnTillions" from my six children. Kelcey, my eldest, taught me about determination. She has always been able do anything she set her mind to. For example, when she decided to go to college to learn to be an art teacher, my first reaction was not very supportive. I said something like, *"Just how many openings do you think there are for art teachers every year? Every art teacher in my experience was in her sixties." You need something more practical."* Her response to my fatherly advice was, *"Well, it's what I want to do."*

Thank God she listened to her own heart and did not listen to me. When Kelcey graduated from Illinois State, she was offered a job as an art teacher after her first interview. To my amazement, Kelcey turned it down because she knew she was good enough to get better offers. They don't teach that kind of confidence and determination in college. After a short while, Kelcey did receive a better offer and has now been enthusiastically teaching art for nine years.

My second daughter, Jancy, taught me about creating what you want. She started college in Florida so she could enjoy the beach, and then transferred to Michigan State to study advertising. Jancy graduated with high honors and took a job with the company with which she had interned. After a few months, she was offered a great job with a major agency in Detroit. However, Jancy became immersed in the corporate world to such a degree that she felt her personal life was suffering, so she created a better job in Denver.

Talk about results. Now, not only does Jancy love her job, she is dating a man she adores and can snowboard all winter. Her attitude is, when your life needs changing, change it.

From my daughter, Carly, I learned about priorities. She just loves nature, so after completing her degree in Forestry at the University of Montana, she went to work for Outward Bound. Her priorities are nature, her friends, family, and then work.

Carly has friends all over the world, but her passion is animals. A few years ago, a bear was stuck in a tree in her front yard. When the animal control experts wanted to shoot the bear with a tranquilizer, Carly was afraid he would be hurt or killed when he fell. So, she made them move her trampoline under the bear to break his fall (you might have seen this on CNN). That's Carly.

My eldest son, Shaunessy, has inspired me from the moment of his birth. He was born six and a half weeks premature. Watching Shaunessy fight for his life during a month in the hospital was quite amazing. When my mother—his grandmother—finally got to hold him, she looked up at me with a tear in her eye and said, *"This was you a heartbeat ago. Where has the time gone?"*

In another heartbeat, Shaunessy achieved his Eagle Scout badge. His project was to produce the play, *All I Really Need to Know, I Learned in Kindergarten,* by Robert Fulghum. He bought the rights to the play, sold the advertising in the program, and assembled the director, actors, and stage crew. Shaunessy then donated all of the profits to the soup kitchen of a local church to feed the needy. Now, he's directing plays at the Milliken University on his quest for his Bachelor of Fine Arts Degree. It's amazing to watch him create his desired results.

My son, Delaney, has taught me perseverance. He is the human equivalent of a train, having one direction and one direction only. If you get in his way you're liable to get run over. I rarely was able to get him to do what I wanted.

In high school, it seemed that he wasn't dedicated to his education. World of Warcraft appeared to be his only interest. Then I found out he had enrolled himself in college. Delaney actually spent his senior year going to high school in the morning and college in the afternoon. Then, he surprised me again by changing colleges and his major. Now he is learning how to create Web pages and DVD menu screens, and possibly even video games.

I introduced my youngest daughter, Shanairra, in the story of her understanding of the power of a positive attitude. From Shanairra comes the lesson of the love of life. She is almost sixteen, and still has her two best friends from age two. She sings, plays the flute, and runs hurdles.

When I would assume my "father role" and discipline her for something, Shanairra would look at me and her bottom lip would quiver. Then twenty minutes later she'd be over it. She would hold up her little pinky finger, grin, and say, "Daddy?" and then get me to do her a favor. Nothing gets in the way of her celebration of life or of giving love. Shanairra is like a reincarnation of my father with this wonderfully unshakeable positive attitude.

One of my most influential mentors was Alexander Everett, the founder of a powerful personal growth company, Mind Dynamics. Alexander was the subject of Jess Stearn's book, *The Power of Alpha Thinking.* He has come to be known as, *"The Teacher of Teachers"* because so many of his students went on to create their own successful training companies.

Some of these leaders include Werner Erhardt of "est" and Landmark Forum, John Hanley of Lifespring, Jim and Jan Quinn of LifeStream, Randy Revell of Context Trainings, Stuart Emery of Actualizations, Howard Nease of Personal Dynamics, Bill Schwartz of The Meditation Institute of Milwaukee, Tom and Jane Willhite of PSI World Seminars, and Robert White of Life Dynamics and ARC. Another man, who has made wonderful use of Alexander's tools and concepts, is Dr. O. Carl Simonton of the Simonton Cancer Center.

Alexander Everett instilled in me the importance of global purpose and individual spirituality. I had thrown out thoughts of spirituality when I got yelled at in Sunday school for asking too many questions. When I met Alexander, I was resistant to the idea of having a higher purpose or God or spirituality or anything reminiscent of my early experiences with religion. Alexander helped me to see clearly that what had been missing in my life was a sense of higher purpose and a connection to what he called "my higher self."

The matriarch of my cadre of mentors was Gram, my father's mother. Everyone called her Gram, except for my brother, Gary, and me. We called her "Sarge," which provides an image of her powerful presence. From Gram I learned that your work and your passion could be the same.

Gram's passion for inspiring people to achieve greater goals was infectious. She worked well into her eighties, enrolling students in our LifeStream Seminars, seven days a week. Everybody loved her. When Lydia Quinn died, hundreds of people showed up to celebrate her amazing life. When it's my turn to go, I want a party like that.

I would not be the same man without my sister, Nancy Cooper (a combination of Mary Tyler Moore and Natalie Wood in attitude and appearance), and my brother, Gary (a comic-sage who is a blend of Mahatma Gandhi and Steve Martin). I have always strived to be like them. Nancy has this attractive elegance that draws people to her like a magnet. Gary has this natural enthusiasm and wisdom that people cannot resist.

There are literally too many people to mention, but I do need to acknowledge my universal role models: Mother Teresa, Buckminster

Fuller, William Penn Patrick, and John Robbins. Each in their own way has inspired individuals to greatness.

Wright

What successes in your own life have you created by using your materials?

Quinn

I'd like to answer within the context of the four components which, when in balance, create success: Physically, Emotionally, Mentally, and Spiritually.

Physically: To use an example most people can relate to, my biggest success physically has to do with my weight. When I was born, I weighed about five pounds. Fifteen years later, I weighed about 160 pounds, having gained about ten to twelve pounds a year.

I continued gaining a little over a pound a year, for the next forty years, with minor fluctuations. Even though I have experimented with diets ranging from all-protein to vegetarian, I have cared little about my weight. I have always been physically fit and healthy.

Then, at age fifty-five, I weighed in at 231 pounds. Suddenly, my perspective changed. I realized that if I kept gaining over a pound a year, by age seventy-two, I would weigh 250 pounds—my dad's weight and age when a heart problem caused his death. Unlike my father, I am blessed with a strong heart. But, I knew if I kept gaining weight, I would eventually be at risk.

In reality, for forty years I had been gaining a little over an ounce a month, effortlessly. I figured the best way to lose weight would have to be just as slow, and just as effortless. After all, I only needed to negate about two ounces a month to shift from gaining weight to losing weight.

Nightly, I began to visualize myself standing on the scale at 199 pounds, and celebrating this desired result. Just as I teach, I focused on two things: 1) changing my thinking and 2) creating my feelings.

Two years later, at a health insurance physical, I weighed in at 222 pounds. Celebration! This was the first time I have ever lost weight and kept it off. I can certainly live with this new habit of losing a little bit every year.

Emotionally: My biggest success emotionally, is the friendship I have with my former wife, Roberta. I think the primary reason our marriage ended in divorce was because I wasn't living the concepts I was teaching. I fell into the classic trap, just like the gardener whose yard is filled with weeds.

It's relatively easy to teach. It's easy to philosophize. But, changing my own behavior was not something that I really wanted to do. I constantly blamed Roberta for our problems and after ten years of marriage, she left. Those endings do not typically heal easily.

Then one day, I woke up to what my resentment was creating. I realized that Roberta was a wonderful mother to our daughters and that we needed to work together for their benefit. After all, I had committed to love, honor, and cherish her until I died. All I really did was keep my original commitment.

My ex-wife will always be the mother of my three older daughters. Truly, one of the greatest blessings of my life is that Roberta has become one of my best friends.

Even more significantly, as a result of changing my attitude, I was able to attract my wife, Christine. Clearly, if I had not, she would have avoided my negativity like the plague.

Mentally: My biggest success came in the midst of one of the most traumatic periods of our time, at least in my memory. That was on Tuesday morning, September 11, 2001. As I watched the turmoil the world was going through, I decided to put my pen to paper and write my book. The working title was, *The Love-Based Leader.*

Up until then, I always "wanted" to write a book, but had never actually begun the process. My father also wanted to write a book, but he died before beginning. I had promised myself at his funeral that it would not happen to me. But, three years later, I still had not begun. So, on that fateful day, I started to write.

To be sure, I was not free of issues and problems. I was not really an author and without funding, I would be too busy to learn.

Well, several people stepped up to the plate and created the funding. Three years later, after changing the title, *Controlling Others For Love And Profit* was introduced to 300 attendees at its kick-off in Niagara Falls, Ontario. I autographed over 1,200 books that night.

Two years later, I recorded my eight-CD personal audio seminar, "Get Over Yourself." I am so very proud of that book and CD. While my father always longed to leave a record of his teachings, he never did so. I have been blessed with the opportunity to leave a concrete legacy of both his work and mine. That is a powerful thought.

Spiritually: My biggest success spiritually is the knowledge that every human being has a "Global Dream." Martin Luther King, Jr.

may have been one of the first to effectively communicate his dream, but we all have one.

My Dream is of a world where all *people treat themselves,* all *other people, and Earth with respect.* I continue to experience the same energy surge each time I speak, write, or even think this phrase.

I created my "Global Impact" outdoor retreat as a system for people to find their Global Dream. Now, over a thousand people can get up in the morning and say, *"My Dream is—"* and see their own vision of a world that works for everyone.

My greatest spiritual victory has been to grow from a man who really only thought about himself to a man who knows that *all* people have their own Global Dream, whether they know it or not. With that knowledge, it is pretty tough to be judgmental of others.

Wright

As soon as I read your bio, I knew this would be one of my questions. Why the outrageous titles for your book and CDs?

Quinn

After twenty-seven years of facilitating personal and professional development seminars, I have come to understand that many people attend personal growth seminars, buy self-help books and CDs, and retain life coaches for one reason: to control someone else.

Certainly, they may be willing to change what they're doing to get others to do what they want, but if it is still about getting others to do what *they* want, it's about control. Whether it is getting someone to treat you with love or give you a job, it's about getting others to do what you want. Even when it's something noble such as wanting to get your kid off drugs, it is still about control.

People don't like to think it's about control, but it is about control. I wanted a title that went to the heart of the matter.

Potential buyers need only to turn to the inside page to learn the true intent of the book: *"Controlling Others for Love and Profit. If you believe that, then you'd better wake up. Controlling others is not the solution—it is the problem."* Regardless of whether they loved or hated the title or cover, they have already gotten their first lesson from the book.

The outrageous title and the blurred cover were designed by a marketing genius who told me, *"If you design it like all the other books, it will disappear on the bookstore shelf."* It is simply designed to attract attention. In reality, no book, regardless of its content, has the ability to help anyone unless it's read—and it will not be read if it's not noticed. Put my book on any bookshelf. It will be noticed.

Wright

Excellent. I like that. Finally, if there was just one thing you would have people take from your work, what would it be?

Quinn

You are greater than you believe you are, and you can create more than you've ever imagined you could—not more than you have achieved, and not more than you have ever wanted, but more than you have ever dreamed you could achieve.

At the end of their lives, many great people have said, *"It really wasn't a big deal. Anybody could have done it!"* Einstein said that about his theory of relativity.

According to Scripture, Jesus Christ said, *"Everything I did, you can do and more"* (John 14:12). Regardless of your beliefs about Him, His teachings were not platitudes designed to flatter us and make us feel good. He spoke what He knew to be the truth.

Most people do not recognize their own greatness and are often too willing to accept other people's perceptions as truth. All information is not truth. When we define ourselves and take responsibility for our lives, there is little we can't achieve.

We are human beings, not human doings. Be a Love-based Leader. It's not what you do, it's how you do it. It's not what others are doing to you, it's what you are doing for them.

There's no big pay-off to playing it safe. Ships in the harbor are safe, but that's not why ships are built. You and I can stay safe by avoiding risk and thus avoiding failure, but that's not why we were born.

Mother Teresa, Buckminster Fuller, and others who made a lasting positive impact with their lives, all had something in common: they defined themselves. Similarly, when we dedicate ourselves to living for a purpose beyond our own comfort, we define ourselves.

The world has enough victims. We need love-based leaders and we need them now. Get over yourself.

Wright

I've enjoyed our conversation. You've shared some valuable information many are seeking.

Quinn

It is an honor to be a part of this project. I am eager to see what the other speakers and authors have written, and I look forward to meeting each of them.

Wright

Thank you so much for being with us on *Speaking of Success.*

Quinn

And I thank you.

About the Author

JAMES ROSWELL QUINN is an international keynote speaker, leadership trainer, business success coach, and author. Since 1979, he has made nearly 1,400 presentations to over 150,000 people in the United States, Canada, New Zealand, Panama, Thailand, Dubai, and the Bahamas.

Quinn's corporate clients have included Walt Disney Feature Animation, Nightingale-Conant Corporation, Toronto Real Estate Board, Lincoln National Life, Pacific Mutual Life, Auckland Multiple Listing Bureau, Microtel Corporation, ReMax Realty, Boise Cascade, UALPA (United Air Lines Pilots Association), Video Law, and several Chicago area banks.

A student of great leaders such as Buckminster Fuller and Mother Teresa, he has coined the phrases: *"Love-based Leader," "Fear-based Reactor," "Pre-acting," "Victimary"* (as opposed to Visionary), *"Impersonal Power,"* and of course, *"Get Over Yourself."*

The body of Quinn's work includes his self-help book, *Controlling Others For Love And Profit,* a DVD of his Toastmasters International address, *Leadership Excellence, The Art of Self-Control,* and his eight-CD personal audio seminar, "Get Over Yourself."

James is a graduate of the University of Southern California. He, his wife, Christine, and the youngest of their six children live in Lake Summerset, Illinois.

James Roswell Quinn
Quinn Incorporated
P.O. Box 766
Durand, IL 61024-0766
815-248-2081
GlobalKeynote@aol.com
http://www.GlobalKeynote.com
http://www.GetOverYourselfStore.com

Chapter 6

JACK CANFIELD

David E. Wright (Wright)

Today we are talking with Jack Canfield. You probably know him as the founder and co-creator of the *New York Times* number one best-selling *Chicken Soup for the Soul* book series. As of 2006 there are sixty-five titles and eighty million copies in print in over thirty-seven languages.

Jack's background includes a BA from Harvard, a master's from the University of Massachusetts, and an Honorary Doctorate from the University of Santa Monica. He has been a high school and university teacher, a workshop facilitator, a psychotherapist, and a leading authority in the area of self-esteem and personal development.

Jack Canfield, welcome to *Speaking of Success.*

Jack Canfield (Canfield)

Thank you, David. It's great to be with you.

Wright

I talked with Mark Victor Hansen a few days ago. He gave you full credit for coming up with the idea of the *Chicken Soup* series. Obviously it's made you an internationally known personality. Other than recognition, has the series changed you personally and if so, how?

Canfield

I would say that it has and I think in a couple of ways. Number one, I read stories all day long of people who've overcome what would feel like insurmountable obstacles. For example, we just did a book *Chicken Soup for the Unsinkable Soul.* There's a story in there about a single mother with three daughters. She contracted a disease and she had to have both of her hands and both of her feet amputated. She got prosthetic devices and was able to learn how to use them. She could cook, drive the car, brush her daughters' hair, get a job, etc. I read that and I thought, "God, what would I ever have to complain and whine and moan about?"

At one level it's just given me a great sense of gratitude and appreciation for everything I have and it has made me less irritable about the little things.

I think the other thing that's happened for me personally is my sphere of influence has changed. By that I mean I was asked, for example, a couple of years ago to be the keynote speaker to the Women's Congressional Caucus. The Caucus is a group that includes all women in America who are members of Congress and who are state senators, governors, and lieutenant governors. I asked what they wanted me to talk about—what topic.

"Whatever you think we need to know to be better legislators," was the reply.

I thought, "Wow, they want me to tell them about what laws they should be making and what would make a better culture." Well, that wouldn't have happened if our books hadn't come out and I hadn't become famous. I think I get to play with people at a higher level and have more influence in the world. That's important to me because my life purpose is inspiring and empowering people to live their highest vision so the world works for everybody. I get to do that on a much bigger level than when I was just a high school teacher back in Chicago.

Wright

I think one of the powerful components of that book series is that you can read a positive story in just a few minutes and come back and revisit it. I know my daughter has three of the books and she just reads them interchangeably. Sometimes I go in her bedroom and she'll be crying and reading one of them. Other times she'll be laughing, so they really are "chicken soup for the soul," aren't they?

Canfield

They really are. In fact we have four books in the *Teenage Soul* series now and a new one coming out at the end of this year. I have a son who's eleven and he has a twelve-year-old friend who's a girl. We have a new book called *Chicken Soup for the Teenage Soul and the Tough Stuff.* It's all about dealing with parents' divorces, teachers who don't understand you, boyfriends who drink and drive, and other issues pertinent to that age group. I asked my son's friend, "Why do you like this book?" (It's our most popular book among teens right now.) She said, "You know, whenever I'm feeling down I read it and it makes me cry and I feel better. Some of the stories make me laugh and some of the stories make me feel more responsible for my life. But basically I just feel like I'm not alone."

One of the people I work with recently said that the books are like a support group between the covers of a book—you can read about other peoples' experiences and realize you're not the only one going through something.

Wright

Jack, with our *Speaking of Success* series we're trying to encourage people in our audience to be better, to live better, and be more fulfilled by reading about the experiences of our writers. Is there anyone or anything in your life that has made a difference for you and helped you to become a better person?

Canfield

Yes and we could do ten books just on that. I'm influenced by people all the time. If I were to go way back I'd have to say one of the key influences in my life was Jesse Jackson when he was still a minister in Chicago. I was teaching in an all black high school there and I went to Jesse Jackson's church with a friend one time. What happened for me was that I saw somebody with a vision. (This was before Martin Luther King was killed and Jesse was of the lieutenants in his organization.) I just saw people trying to make the world work better for a certain segment of the population. I was inspired by that kind of visionary belief that it's possible to make change.

Later on, John F. Kennedy was a hero of mine. I was very much inspired by him.

Another is a therapist by the name of Robert Resnick. He was my therapist for two years. He taught me a little formula called E + R = O that stands for Events + Response = Outcome. He said, "If you don't like your outcomes quit blaming the events and start changing your responses." One of his favorite phrases was, "If the grass on the other side of the fence looks greener, start watering your own lawn more."

I think he helped me get off any kind of self-pity I might have had because I had parents who were alcoholics. It would have been very easy to blame them for problems I might have had. They weren't very successful or rich; I was surrounded by people who were and I felt like, "God, what if I'd had parents like they had? I could have been a lot better." He just got me off that whole notion and made me realize the hand you were dealt is the hand you've got to play and take responsibility for who you are and quit complaining and blaming others and get on with your life. That was a turning point for me.

I'd say the last person who really affected me big time was a guy named W. Clement Stone who was a self-made multi-millionaire in Chicago. He taught me that success is not a four-letter word—it's nothing to be ashamed of—and you ought to go for it. He said, "The best thing you can do for the poor is not be one of them." Be a model for what it is to live a successful life. So I learned from him the principles of success and that's what I've been teaching now for more than thirty years.

Wright

He was an entrepreneur in the insurance industry, wasn't he?

Canfield

He was. He had combined insurance. When I worked for him he was worth 600 million dollars and that was before the dot.com millionaires came along in Silicon Valley. He just knew more about success. He was a good friend of Napoleon Hill (author of *Think and Grow Rich)* and he was a fabulous mentor. I really learned a lot from him.

Wright

I miss some of the men I listened to when I was a young salesman coming up and he was one of them. Napoleon Hill was another one as was Dr. Peale. All of their writings made me who I am today. I'm glad I had that opportunity.

Canfield

One speaker whose name you probably will remember, Charlie "Tremendous" Jones, says, "Who we are is a result of the books we read and the people we hang out with." I think that's so true and that's why I tell people, "If you want to have high self-esteem, hang out with people who have high self-esteem. If you want to be more spiritual, hang out with spiritual people." We're always telling our children, "Don't hang out with those kids." The reason we don't want them to is because we know how influential people are with each other. I think we need to give ourselves the same advice. Who are we hanging out with? We can hang out with them in books, cassette tapes, CDs, radio shows, and in person.

Wright

One of my favorites was a fellow named Bill Gove from Florida. I talked with him about three or four years ago. He's retired now. His mind is still as quick as it ever was. I thought he was one of the greatest speakers I had ever heard.

What do you think makes up a great mentor? In other words, are there characteristics that mentors seem to have in common?

Canfield

I think there are two obvious ones. I think mentors have to have the time to do it and the willingness to do it. I also think they need to be people who are doing something you want to do. W. Clement Stone used to tell me, "If you want to be rich, hang out with rich people. Watch what they do, eat what they eat, dress the way they dress. Try it on." He wasn't suggesting that you give up your authentic self, but he was pointing out that rich people probably have habits that you don't have and you should study them.

I always ask salespeople in an organization, "Who are the top two or three in your organization?" I tell them to start taking them out to lunch and dinner and for a drink and finding out what they do. Ask them, "What's your secret?" Nine times out of ten they'll be willing to tell you.

This goes back to what we said earlier about asking. I'll go into corporations and I'll say, "Who are the top ten people?" They'll all tell me and I'll say, "Did you ever ask them what they do different than you?"

"No," they'll reply.

"Why not?"

"Well, they might not want to tell me."

"How do you know? Did you ever ask them? All they can do is say no. You'll be no worse off than you are now."

So I think with mentors you just look at people who seem to be living the life you want to live and achieving the results you want to achieve.

What we say in our book is when that you approach a mentor they're probably busy and successful and so they haven't got a lot of time. Just ask, "Can I talk to you for ten minutes every month?" If I know it's only going to be ten minutes I'll probably say yes. The neat thing is if I like you I'll always give you more than ten minutes, but that ten minutes gets you in the door.

Wright

In the future are there any more Jack Canfield books authored singularly?

Canfield

One of my books includes the formula I mentioned earlier: E + R = O. I just felt I wanted to get that out there because every time I give a speech and I talk about that the whole room gets so quiet that you could hear a pin drop—I can tell people are really getting value. Then I'm going to do a series of books on the principles of success. I've got about 150 of them that I've identified over the years. I have a book down the road I want to do that's called *No More Put-Downs,* which is a book probably aimed mostly at parents, teacher and managers. There's a culture we have now of put-down humor. Whether it's *Married With Children* or *All in the Family,* there's that characteristic of macho put-down humor. There's research now showing how bad it is for kids' self-esteem when the coaches do it so I want to get that message out there as well.

Wright

It's really not that funny, is it?

Canfield

No, we'll laugh it off because we don't want to look like we're a wimp but underneath we're hurt. The research now shows that you're better off breaking a child's bones than you are breaking their spirit. A bone will heal much more quickly than their emotional spirit will.

Wright

I remember recently reading a survey where people listed the top five people who had influenced them. I've tried it on a couple of groups at church and in other places. In my case, and in the survey, approximately three out of the top five are always teachers. I wonder if that's going to be the same in the next decade.

Canfield

I think that's probably because as children we're at our most formative years. We actually spend more time with our teachers than we do with our parents. Research shows that the average parent only interacts verbally with each of their children only about eight and a half minutes a day. Yet at school they're interacting with their teachers for anywhere from six to eight hours depending on how long the school day is, including coaches, chorus directors, etc.

I think that in almost everybody's life there's been that one teacher who loved him or her as a human being—an individual—not just one of the many students the teacher was supposed to fill full of History and English. That teacher believed in you and inspired you.

Les Brown is one of the great motivational speakers in the world. If it hadn't been for one teacher who said, "I think you can do more than be in a special ed. class. I think you're the one," he'd probably still be cutting grass in the median strip of the highways in Florida instead of being a $35,000-a-talk speaker.

Wright

I had a conversation one time with Les. He told me about this wonderful teacher who discovered Les was dyslexic. Everybody else called him dumb and this one lady just took him under her wing and had him tested. His entire life changed because of her interest in him.

Canfield

I'm on the board of advisors of the Dyslexic Awareness Resource Center here in Santa Barbara. The reason is because I taught high school with a lot of kids who were called at-risk—kids who would end up in gangs and so forth. What we found over and over was that about 78 percent of all the kids in the juvenile detention centers in Chicago were kids who had learning disabilities—primarily dyslexia—but there were others as well. They were never diagnosed and they weren't doing well in school so they'd drop out. As soon as a student drops out of school he or she becomes subject to the influence of gangs and other kinds of criminal and drug linked activities. If these kids had been diagnosed earlier we'd get rid of a large amount of the juvenile crime in America because there are a lot of really good programs that can teach dyslexics to read and excel in school.

Wright

My wife is a teacher and she brings home stories that are heartbreaking about parents not being as concerned with their children as they used to be, or at least not as helpful as they used to be. Did you find that to be a problem when you were teaching?

Canfield

It depends on what kind of district you're in. If it's a poor district the parents could be on drugs, alcoholics, and basically just not available. If you're in a really high rent district the parents not available because they're both working, coming home tired, they're jet-setters, or they're working late at the office because they're workaholics. Sometimes it just legitimately takes two paychecks to pay the rent anymore.

I find that the majority of parents care but often they don't know what to do. They don't know how to discipline their children. They don't know how to help them with their homework. They can't pass on skills that they never acquired themselves. Unfortunately, the trend tends to be like a chain letter. The people with the least amount of skills tend to have the most number of children. The other thing is that you get crack babies (infants born addicted to crack cocaine because of the mother's addiction). In Los Angeles one out of every ten babies born is a crack baby.

Wright

That's unbelievable.

Canfield

Yes and another statistic is that by the time 50 percent of the kids are twelve years old they have started experimenting with alcohol. I see a lot of that in the Bible belt. The problem is not the big city, urban designer drugs but alcoholism. Another thing you get, unfortunately, is a lot of let's call it familial violence—kids getting beat up, parents who drink and then explode—child abuse and sexual abuse. You see a lot of that.

Wright

Most people are fascinated by these television shows about being a survivor. What has been the greatest comeback that you have made from adversity in your career or in your life?

Canfield

You know it's funny, I don't think I've had a lot of major failures and setbacks where I had to start over. My life's been on an intentional curve. But I do have a lot of challenges. Mark and I are always setting goals that challenge us. We always say, "The purpose of setting a really big goal is not so that you can achieve it so much, but it's who you become in the process of achieving it." A friend of mine, Jim Rohn, says, "You want to set goals big enough so that in the process of achieving them you become someone worth being."

I think that to be a millionaire is nice but so what? People make the money and then they lose it. People get the big houses and then they burn down, or Silicon Valley goes belly up and all of a sudden they don't have a big house anymore. But who you became in the process of learning how to do that can never be taken away from you. So what we do is constantly put big challenges in front of us.

We have a book called *Chicken Soup for the Teacher's Soul.* (You'll have to make sure to get a copy for your wife.) I was a teacher and a teacher trainer for years. But because of the success of the *Chicken Soup* books I haven't been in the education world that much. I've got to go out and relearn how do I market to that world? I met with a Superintendent of Schools. I met with a guy named Jason Dorsey who's one of the number one consultants in the world in that area. I found out who has the best selling book in that area. I sat down with his wife for a day and talked about her marketing approaches.

I believe that if you face any kind of adversity, whether losing your job, your spouse dies, you get divorced, you're in an accident like Christopher Reeves and become paralyzed, or whatever, you simply do what you have to do. You find out who's already handled the problem and how did they've handled it. Then you get the support you need to get through it by their example. Whether it's a counselor in your church or you go on a retreat or you read the Bible, you do something that gives you the support you need to get to the other end.

You also have to know what the end is that you want to have. Do you want to be remarried? Do you just want to have a job and be a single mom? What is it? If you reach out and ask for support I think you'll get help. People really like to help other people. They're not always available because sometimes they're going through problems also; but there's always someone with a helping hand.

Often I think we let our pride get in the way. We let our stubbornness get in the way. We let our belief in how the world should be interfere and get in our way instead of dealing with how the world is. When we get that out of that way then we can start doing that which we need to do to get where we need to go.

Wright

If you could have a platform and tell our audience something you feel that would help or encourage them, what would you say?

Canfield

I'd say number one is to believe in yourself, believe in your dreams, and trust your feelings. I think too many people are trained wrong when they're little kids. For example, when kids are mad at their daddy they're told, "You're not mad at your Daddy."

They say, "Gee, I thought I was."

Or the kid says, "That's going to hurt," and the doctor says, "No it's not." Then they give you the shot and it hurts. They say, "See that didn't hurt, did it?" When that happened to you as a kid, you started to not trust yourself.

You may have asked your mom, "Are you upset?" and she says, "No," but she really was. So you stop learning to trust your perception.

I tell this story over and over. There are hundreds of people I've met who've come from upper class families where they make big incomes and the dad's a doctor. The kid wants to be a mechanic and work in an auto shop because that's what he loves. The family says, "That's beneath us. You can't do that." So the kid ends up being an anesthesiologist killing three people because he's not paying attention. What he really wants to do is tinker with cars. I tell people you've got to trust your own feelings, your own motivations, what turns you on, what you want to do, what makes you feel good, and quit worrying about what other people say, think, and want for you.

Decide what you want for yourself and then do what you need to do to go about getting it. It takes work.

I read a book a week minimum and at the end of the year I've read fifty-two books. We're talking about professional books—books on self-help, finances, psychology, parenting, and so forth. At the end of ten years I've read 520 books. That puts me in the top 1 percent of people knowing important information in this country. But most people are spending their time watching television.

When I went to work for W. Clement Stone, he told me, "I want you to cut out one hour a day of television."

"Okay," I said, "what do I do with it?"

"Read," he said.

He told me what kind of books to read. He said, "At the end of a year you'll have spent 365 hours reading. Divide that by a forty-hour work week and that's nine and a half weeks of education every year."

I thought, "Wow, that's two months." It was like going back to summer school.

As a result of his advice I have close to 8,000 books in my library. The reason I'm involved in this book project instead of someone else is that people like me, Jim Rohn, Les Brown, and you read a lot. We listen to tapes and we go to seminars. That's why we're the people with the information.

I always say that your raise becomes effective when you do. You'll become more effective as you gain more skills, more insight, and more knowledge.

Wright

Jack, I have watched your career for over a decade and your accomplishments are just outstanding. But your humanitarian efforts are really what impress me. I think that you're doing great things not only in California, but all over the country.

Canfield

It's true. In addition to all of the work we do, we pick one to three charities and we've given away over six million dollars in the last eight years, along with our publisher who matches every penny we give away. We've planted over a million trees in Yosemite National Park. We've bought hundreds of thousands of cataract operations in third world countries. We've contributed to the Red Cross, the Humane Society, and on it goes. It feels like a real blessing to be able to make that kind of a contribution to the world.

Wright

Today we have been talking with Jack Canfield, founder and co-creator of the *Chicken Soup for the Soul* book series. As of 2006, there are sixty-five titles and eighty million copies in print in over thirty-seven <u>languages</u>.

Canfield

The most recent book is *The Success Principles*. In it I share sixty-four principles that other people and I have utilized to achieve great levels of success.

In 2002 we published *Chicken Soup for the Soul of America*. It includes stories that grew out of 9/11 and is a real healing book for our nation. I would encourage readers to get a copy and share it with their families.

Wright

I will stand in line to get one of those. Thank you so much being with us on *Speaking of Success.*

About The Author

JACK CANFIELD is one of America's leading experts on developing self-esteem and peak performance. A dynamic and entertaining speaker, as well as a highly sought-after trainer, he has a wonderful ability to inform and inspire audiences toward developing their own human potential and personal effectiveness.

Jack Canfield is most well-known for the *Chicken Soup for the Soul* series, which he co-authored with Mark Victor Hansen, and for his audio programs about building high self-esteem. Jack is the founder of Self-Esteem Seminars, located in Santa Barbara, California, which trains entrepreneurs, educators, corporate leaders, and employees how to accelerate the achievement of their personal and professional goals. Jack is also the founder of The Foundation for Self Esteem, located in Culver City, California, which provides self-esteem resources and training to social workers, welfare recipients, and human resource professionals.

Jack graduated from Harvard in 1966, received his ME degree at the university of Massachusetts in 1973, and earned an Honorary Doctorate from the University of Santa Monica. He has been a high school and university teacher, a workshop facilitator, a psychotherapist, and a leading authority in the area of self-esteem and personal development.

As a result of his work with prisoners, welfare recipients, and inner-city youth, Jack was appointed by the state legislature to the California Task Force to Promote Self-Esteem and Personal and Social Responsibility. He also served on the board of trustees of the National Council for Self-Esteem.

Jack Canfield
Worldwide Headquarters
The Jack Canfield Companies
P.O. Box 30880
Santa Barbara, CA 93130
Phone: 805.563.2935
Fax: 805.563.2945
www.jackcanfield.com

Chapter 7

TERRY DAUGHERTY

THE INTERVIEW

David Wright (Wright)

Dr. Terry Daugherty is a highly respected orthodontist and business entrepreneur in the Dallas area. Developing a world-class practice that combined technical, people, and business excellence, he created a system for multiplying the concept in other practices through his simple systems and processes.

He is a National Speakers Association member, author, coach, consultant, and inspiring speaker for various companies nationwide. The principles of business success process, growth strategies, relational psychology, and inspirational leadership are the core of his message.

Dr. Daugherty assists business leaders in getting the most out of their businesses, their teams, and themselves. Additionally, he helps team (staff) members become *Valued Partners*™ so that they can get the most out of their careers, focusing on a high result, low stress approach.

Terry, how do you define success?

Dr. Terry Daugherty (Daugherty)

I heard it said years ago that "success is the progressive realization of worthwhile goals." Worthwhile goals to me would be to maximize my life balance goals:

- Worship
- Family
- Work
- Play

"Worship" would be one's spiritual life. "Family" covers family, friends, and people relationships. "Work" would include one's job (i.e., work, livelihood), one's personal family business, or career. "Play" would be other activities and interests as well as health and fitness issues. Success for most people is to passionately pursue quality goals in these areas with some balance.

I believe that without any one of these quadrants we won't be as happy as we could be, in the long-term. Most people I know who are highly successful say they are out of balance, especially when they are accelerating their success in any one area. Seldom are we in balance all the time. Whatever we are working on, for brief periods of time, takes precedence over the others in order to accelerate growth in the area that has our attention at that time. So a single-minded focus at times helps us accelerate our success in a particular area, such as writing a book or creating a seminar.

I get temporarily out of balance as most people do. However, if I stay unbalanced, over time it will be detrimental to my overall life success.

Wright

What are some obstacles you see that people face in becoming successful?

Daugherty

I believe that most people lack a strong belief in themselves and a sense of purpose in their life. Said another way, they don't have a positive self-image. I think some of that is a result of not seeing God's hand in the possibilities for their life's purpose. Whatever the reason, this reduces the chances that someone will take the next important step to see and create a vision for what success looks like to them. Most don't spend enough focused time looking within and determining what they really want to become in life or business. This causes us to be what Zig Ziglar would call a "wondering generality rather than a meaningful specific."

Most are influenced by the actions or words of friends and sometimes family, thus never rise to the level they are capable of achieving. There are still others who use friends and family as a reason why they can't or don't become what they want to become. However, I believe that most just don't take the time to focus and discover what they really want or what they are capable of becoming.

It is interesting to me that whether you rise above or stay below your success potential, the same circumstances can inspire either. For example, some rise above because they had a disadvantaged childhood, yet others use that as the reason for not rising above their circumstances. Sometimes the highly advantaged say that having too much money counteracted motivation for them to work hard toward success. Interesting dichotomy!

One thing is certain, a clear purpose and vision for what you want to accomplish in life or for that matter business, creates the desire to see the vision become a reality. The desire is fueled further by having goals that are applied to the vision as benchmarks for instance. This narrows the focus of actions that you are going to take. In the journey to achieve the goals, a positive attitude is a key to both maintaining discipline and persistence toward that goal achievement.

Attitude is critical to creating the *"Power of We™,"* because it infects others, especially if it is highly passionate. A positive attitude is a powerful ingredient in creating a unified and passionate team when it comes to business. It multiplies the ripple effect and becomes self-perpetuating. This sort of leadership is powerfully transparent and emotionally intelligent. It creates energy and focus for the perpetuation of success. Internally generated and externally perceived!

Wright

Will you tell our readers a little bit about what drives you to be successful?

Daugherty

To know that is to know a little of my personal history. I had a very successful business in Dallas Texas and sold it and moved to Hilton Head, South Carolina, in 1998. I thought retiring early would be such a great thing and the fulfillment of a dream of getting to retire with the financial freedom to do whatever I wanted to do each day.

Wow! I was shocked to realize that I got really bored after about six months! I worked on my golf game, sailed in the South Pacific, and traveled to other countries for a couple of months at a time to play and see things I've never seen. I was shocked to find that at the end of the day, I was asking myself the question, "Shouldn't I be doing something more important with my life?"

I realized that having more "spare time" didn't necessarily equate to "more fulfillment" in life. I felt an internal need to make a contribution. People called and asked me to consult for them—to help in advancing their business growth, people harmony, and simplify the quest they had for success. I did so and soon after started a consulting company with my brother, Dave, called Daugherty Consulting.

In my case, I have reinvented the definition and direction of success for myself. I am now a speaker, author, and consultant. What drives me to continue to make an impact in the lives of business leaders, team members, and their companies? I wanted to change things and have the audacity to really make an impact!

My purpose with my company is to assist business leaders get the most out of themselves and their people in their business life, speaking and coaching the fundamentals and how to build them "effectively. Further, my purpose is also to assist people in all career levels become *Valued Partners*™ in their work lives. Said another way, I want to assist people in achieving career happiness through the process of becoming "knowledgeable workers" who are passionate about their work and the company that employs them—to make a real contribution! In doing so, their personal life will be more fulfilling, enthusiastic, and ultimately more prosperous.

Wright

Is it important to balance your success in your life?

Daugherty

In my opinion, one key for success in life is balance! A balance in life includes Worship, Family, Work, and Play as I said before. That's what I strive for and I believe most people are happier when they have these in balance. We have all seen that you can really gain "worldly success" and lose your core happiness in life in the process. The good news is that you can have it all. In fact, I find that when people aren't producing the results they want in life, usually they are repeatedly out of balance in one or more of those areas. From the boardroom to the mailroom, the fundamental four apply. The intensity and focus will be different, yet for business success it helps to connect the dots of success principals in a company.

Wright

How do you balance your success in life?

Daugherty

I try to keep an awareness of what is in balance in my life and be mindful of when I will temporarily be out of balance so that I can work around this issue and eventually get back into better balance. Don't get me wrong, I get out of balance frequently—I just challenge myself to reorient to what is important to my overall personal success and fulfillment. I believe that I am more effective in all areas when I am in overall balance.

Wright

What is the message you want people to hear so that they can learn from your success?

Daugherty

Simply, that you can have the life you want—you can live "your dream"—if you will dare to recognize what you really want, then take charge of your life actions to get success for you. I commonly use the phrase, "Have the audacity." To me this term means to have the boldness, daring, courage, or maybe the "insanity" to believe that you were created to do something really special on this planet—to live a successful life, whatever that is for you. It's not necessarily about money; it's about having a mission and purpose to make a difference. *No,* better yet it's more about making an *impact* with your life.

Business success involves taking charge or "making a change" and being responsible for getting your business or career the way you want it to be. Be courageous and disciplined in your business vision. Stand for and maintain integrity, humility, and gratefulness in all your dealings.

As you go about crafting your dream business you must develop a clear concept of that business exactly as you want it to be—your business vision. Innovate and enhance your business with quality and effectiveness that will differentiate you in the marketplace.

If you don't have a business then consider yourself the business—such as a team member, a staff member, or employee. Work on a "you" that is impossible to replace. You add so much value to the customers and the organization that someone truly exceptional would have to be hired to fill your shoes. Be a stepping-stone rather than a stumbling block with others on your team—be a *Valued Partner™*.

Be the kind of person you respect in business—one who respects and empathizes with others and is a passion builder and unifier in all that you do in the company. When adversity comes, take the "high road" with perseverance and adaptability as your tools for moving positively forward. Be a real "spark plug" in the business! You don't have to be extravagant to give a smile and kind word to your teammates and customers to brighten their day. It's contagious!

Wright

Are there people who have served as role models along your path to success?

Daugherty

Many! First, the example shown by my dad (Charlie Daugherty), who really never achieved much financial success, yet was the greatest man I have ever met. I learned more from my father, mostly by his example, than I ever learned from people with post-graduate degrees or any of my mentors. He loves people and is a real "giver" into the emotional bank account of people's lives with his caring and his sincere desire to help people. He has great values, character, compassion, and caring. He embodies these things in his actions. Oh, did I leave out his common sense, people brilliance, and emotional intelligence? He had great success even without financial success.

Money was in short as a child. I felt insecure about whether we would have enough to "make it." I incorporated a desire to not be poor when I grew up; I probably even had a little fear of failure as well. Fear was a driver behind some of my actions until I realized how to have an abundance mentality.

The concept that I call "Audacity" came through my dad to me. He basically said that you can do anything in life you want to do if you just trust God, have the Audacity to believe it is possible for you, persevere when life gets tough, and never forget to help others in their journey.

The Bible is ranked first to me because it is the rock upon which everything else in life is built for the power, potential, and possibilities that insure true success in life—a truth I didn't know enough about in my early days and one that hopefully I'm learning more now. Finally, when I read Napoleon Hill's book, *"Think and Grow Rich,"* it was very helpful to me at an important time in my life. Zig Zigler, Jim Rohn, and Tony Robbins' work were all helpful and added ideas, energy, and belief in what was possible for me and my "Team" for that matter.

Wright
You give credit to mentors such as your dad, Zig Ziglar, Jim Rohn, Tony Robbins, and others in helping you succeed. How can people help other people succeed?

Daugherty
We can help other people succeed if we can help them see the possibilities that already exist within themselves. This will often help overcome the inertia of mediocrity in our lives. We can share our experiences with others and try to infect them with the desire and passion for seeing and perusing their dream lives.

Most successful people I have met have had someone in their past who was a mentor or significant role model who directly or indirectly influenced them to have a better business life. These people are mostly humble, grateful, and willing to help others succeed. Mentoring is like a debt we owe to those who, like us, really want to know how to become successful. Some have overcome seemingly impossible or improbable odds to be very successful. I want to give back the blessings that my mentors and role models have generously given me.

As an example, when I was in high school I was an average or below average student. A well meaning school counselor told me that I needed to continue to be good at athletics because I had an average IQ and had limited academic potential. He was my football coach.

I got drafted into military service in my second year of college. While in the military, I took some tests that showed that I had an aptitude for medicine and science. I really liked the field of medicine and became a medic. Many of the doctors I worked with encouraged me to go back to school and become a doctor. I returned to school, became an honor student, and graduated number one in my class. Why? Because someone helped me believe I could and I persevered and overcame adversities to fulfill my new vision for my career. I created a practice that was in the top 1 percent of that business. I didn't raise my intelligence level—I raised my level of faith in what was possible. By some miracle someone helped me see what I hadn't seen in myself before.

The point is that we must filter the comments we receive and guard our minds from negative influences. Failures from our past, the critical words and actions from others need not deter us. We must never allow another person to cause us to have lower self-esteem. IQ is not the defining factor in creating or diminishing success in life. It's nice to be brilliant, yet brilliance is not the measure of whether or not you should pursue your dream and become highly successful.

I am passionate about helping people in all levels of business become inspired, to be all that they were meant to be, and have passion about doing so.

I love speaking to high school students who feel average or below average. I want to inspire them to step up and be the "great one" that God meant for them to be. Success at anything requires all the ingredients we mentioned above. As Zig Ziglar frequently said, "The elevator to the top is out of order; you must take the stairs and work at it in order to get to the top." What a great feeling to have overcome adversity on the way to becoming a better you and me!

Wright

What was the biggest contribution to your business success?

Daugherty

From here on I will focus on business success more so than personal success. As you know, I believe the same ingredients go into both. The principals apply equally for the business owner or those with a career working within a company.

When I learned how to create a successful business I found the following concepts to be important: Having a clear vision for what I want the business to be like is important. I simply fantasize or dream about having it exactly and clearly the way I want it to be. I pose no limitations upon myself and the business. I must believe it is possible, and then I envision it—picture and feel it—in my heart and spirit before I can create it in the real world.

Napoleon Hill said, "What the mind of man can believe and conceive, it can achieve." I call this the "laser beam effect." As for me, I really caught hold of that concept—I got it! That has made a huge difference in my life.

Crystal clear vision is the "guidance system" of personal and business success. Lack of a vision leads to confusing activity with accomplishment. This can lead to spending lots of life's precious time in just doing something rather than doing something important. Most people do what seems urgent to them at the moment, lacking direction and the discipline to do what is really important to creating success.

How it worked for me is that once I believed and then clearly conceived, I followed that by incorporating an even greater level of belief. Then the desire showed up, which lead to effective planning. In the planning stage, I looked at "how I could make it really happen." This caused me to fully realize that other people would have to be the "lever" to create a ripple effect in business, which causes a higher level of success. This led me to the need to understand how to become a good leader and coach to my team so that we could all succeed together. It's about the concept of "We" succeeding or what I call "The Power of We."

When you have a team working in unity, all things are possible in your business. This process took it from the subconscious mind to conscious reality for me in business. This is what I now call "*The Power of We™*," and the "We" for me was the biggest contribution to my success. This is also why I call highly competent and passionate team members *"Valued Partners™."* They are clearly valuable in partnering in the success of any endeavor, and need to be seen as valued and treated as such in a company. This concept that I teach is critical and it is the "jet fuel" for good businesses that want to become world class.

What I did was to envision what I wanted the business to be like exactly. I used the "laser beam theory," then I planned it and created the environment and training to develop these *"Valued Partners™"* to leverage the success.

Statisticians say more than 90 percent of the workers on the planet are either negative or neutral about their jobs. That is a tragic misuse of human potential. How wonderful it would be if people could come to work excited about their work, leave with the feeling that they contributed to something worthwhile, and made a difference while at work that day. Most people clearly have not unlocked that feeling in themselves or others in the workplace. Most people, to one degree or another, are just PI-POs—punch in and punch outs. Successful businesses at world-class levels don't have "punchers," they have passionate producing partners.

In my business, I wanted to change that so that our team would be a "band of radicals" who were unstoppable—the "We Force" as I call them. We found a way to have an inspirational vision and desire to become the best at what we did. This created energy, enthusiasm, and passion for the work we did and caused us to want to be high level "knowledge workers." Part of that knowledge was to increase our emotional intelligence in our interactions with each other and the people we served. That is one of our success secrets!

I feel that high-level success in any business is dependent upon our ability to have the "Audacity" to conceive and believe our vision, with leadership skills to leverage our talents and vision through people into the focused and laser-like "Power of We."

Wright

Tell me about what you refer to as the Fundamental Four™ in the success process.

Daugherty

This is a key concept to me. I have given this great study and observation over time. This has worked well for me and others I have consulted for and coached. The Fundamental Four is a foundational concept for business success. Yet, as is usually true, it can be translated into a model for any successful endeavor, not just business.

Inspirational leadership is simple, yet quite rare. It is about communicating with your people concerning where you are taking the business and what behaviors will get the team there successfully. It is not about being charismatic, extroverted, or overly exciting as a person. It is about building a solid, yet evolving foundation in four fundamental areas. Your team becomes inspired with purpose and direction when they know where you want to take the business, what is expected of them, and how they can meet those expectations.

By clarifying the "Fundamental Four™"—vision, leadership, business culture, and "Valued Partners™"—you will create a foundation or platform for your unique business. This leader-designed platform starts everything rolling along the right track for your business. You set in motion a Ripple Effect that will define your company's potential into the future.

The Fundamental Four are:

- Vision—translated through your
- Leadership—into a
- Culture—we developed through
- Valued Partners.

Once established the process becomes team-driven. They support, maintain, and sustain the ongoing efforts necessary to produce results.

Simply put, it all starts with getting a "grip" on your personal Vision for your life and business. The reality is that your vision is the "guidance system" that helps you lead and manage effectively. You identify the kind of Leadership that is needed to create what you really want. Generally, these two steps require someone from outside your business to help you and get clarity. Often that is where we start as a coaching consultant.

Then share your Vision with your team verbally—proclaim it! Make it crystal clear! Share how everyone has a part and how they can all reach their best career goals as a team. Talk with the team about how "we all" can make the business a success for all of us.

Leadership is not difficult if we understand how it works and how it can be simplified. One way is through developing a positive and productive business culture. As businesses we must have actions and behaviors that are aligned with and support our business vision. It is important that we conduct business around what "we value" and how it shows up in how "we" behave in the company. It also has to do with what we expect from each other around quality, team, and client relationships, and how we are perceived in our business image. This is so important, so perpetuating, and powerful when hiring new team members and getting buy-in as to how your team sees its success as a business.

"What most team members want is inspirational leadership with clear direction and expectations! They want—even desire—to exceed expectations and contribute at a higher level. Only the leader can set the standard and model these behaviors of success," says Dave Daugherty, co-founder of Daugherty Consulting.

In the highly effective businesses of our clients, we coach team members to become "*Valued Partners™.*" *Valued Partners™* are highly developed "knowledge workers" who are fully engaged, career oriented, and passionate about the work and the business they are a valuable part of.

The bottom line is you have to envision and create the environment, set the expectations, and hire/develop people into these roles within your business. If you work on this principle you will reap huge benefits personally and professionally for you and the entire team. This leverages the concept of the "*Power of We™.*"

To simplify, yet heighten success in relationships (both internal and external), is critical. A key factor for every leader is to become aware of and increase mastery in a field called Emotional Intelligence (EI). The reason is that EI is twice as important as "cognitive or technical abilities" in predicting employee performance. It accounts for more than 75 percent of star performance in top leaders, according to Daniel Goleman's research at Harvard University.

Emotional Intelligence pays big dividends. How we manage relationships is significantly based upon how aware we are of our own dynamics and our impact on others. Increasing our awareness, learning simple, self-management techniques, and simplifying the people management aspect of our business will yield enormous results in our companies.

These Core Principals that we at Daugherty Consulting call the Foundational Four are simple and they drive the effectiveness and simplicity of the other business principles.

Wright

Why do you feel that so many business leaders don't really have a clear vision for themselves or their business?

Daugherty

I believe that many business leaders work much more "in" their business than working "on" their business. This sets up a situation where they become immersed in and focused on doing the business, and not focusing on being the cultural leader, the business entrepreneur, and the strategist of the business. Said another way, this causes business "leaders" to be caught up in details and not spend enough time on conceiving, strategizing, and leveraging the business model that will ultimately lead to higher success. This is especially true when leaders in small businesses are key workers in the business as well. This is an inherent problem in most small business situations.

The thinking time to "get and keep in touch" with their vision for the enterprise and not just the product seems illusive and foreign to them. This step seems too "non-productive" for many leaders, so it doesn't get priority time or focused thought and attention. This is a mistake and lessens the organizational leveraging effectiveness of the team.

Wright

You seem to feel strongly about this issue; expand on this a little. Why is it so important in your opinion?

Daugherty

It's important because it is in "glaring" need for attention in most businesses. It is always present in the study of great business leaders and world-class companies—highly successful businesses. Research on world-class businesses and the work of my esteemed co-authors in this book, Stephen Covey, Ken Blanchard, Jack Canfield, and most others espouse the same basic observations.

It starts with a leader who has the foresight, courage, and discipline to envision the business clearly and crisply in the way they want it to ideally be. Leaders infused with a clear picture of the dream business in their minds cause it to become a passion and desire in their hearts. Successful leaders then have the leadership skills to make it real in the hearts and minds of the team members through inspirational leadership and Emotional Intelligence (EI). Thus the business Culture is instilled in the team's attitudes and behaviors. The successful leader then leverages the doing, implementation, and advancement of the vision through his team. The leader then leverages the success through being the designer-facilitator of the business success.

When the leader reaches full leverage potential he or she will have developed high-level *Valued Partners*™ that I mentioned above. This process that further accelerates business success is accomplished through collaborative leadership by the *Valued Partners*™ and the *Power of We*™ principles. You might say it is leader-designed and team-driven success. That's when you create a "bullet proof" company with an uncommon level of success. The top leadership is mostly working *on* the business, and *Valued Partners*™ are all working mostly *in* the business. All are collaborators in the quest for experiencing uncommon success.

Wright

Why did you choose to start speaking and consulting?

Daugherty

I didn't choose it, it chose me! Others wanted to see what my team and I were doing when I was building a highly successful business model. That success in the business was palpable; our passion was contagious. One of our slogans, "Have Passion and Pass-It-On!" was a business battle cry.

Eventually I was asked to share the success system with other business leaders and their teams. This sharing process got me interested in becoming an accomplished speaker in order to more effectively infect others with my passion for the message—to Pass-It-On. When I sold my businesses I was asked to consult and speak and decided that I wanted to spread my concept through speaking, writing, and consulting. The message translates to any business situation.

My heart is with people in all areas of the company. I am passionate about their achieving a fuller life through reaching their potential. I can possibly be the spark that ignites the passion and potential that resides within every one of us and it causes them to live more successful and fulfilling lives.

Wright

You mentioned *The Power of We*™. Would you touch on that for a moment?

Daugherty

I realized early in my business the *Power of We*™. The experience of going from being a worker in a business with poor leadership to working for a leader with exceptional skills in empowering and inspiring real team spirit changed my life. As mentioned earlier, it inspired me to be the best me I could be and to go beyond my potential. It started a new dream in me, and before long I was in the position to Pass-It-On. I took those experiences into my own business and applied those "we power" principles. I realized there was a great need for these skills in business.

I ask business leaders this question frequently: "What percent of your employees are tens, meaning engaged and committed to your business?" The answer averages about 30 percent. It shouldn't be a surprise—most research shows that few people even enjoy their jobs let alone have a passion for the success of the company.

I firmly believe that most workers are just waiting for a leader to come along with a vision so powerful that they will get swept off their feet and become passionate about and engaged in their work. Obviously that has power to create great success in business—right?

I learned how to get my vision clear and transfer the vision to my team more effectively. Then I assist them in seeing how to enhance their careers and collaborate within and outside of our business in order to leverage our success. My brother, Dave, and I co-developed a system to turn team members into *Valued Partners™*. The result was a high result, low stress model for business success.

Wright

You frequently use the term "have Passion and Pass-it-on." What do you mean by that and why is it important to personal and business success?

Daugherty

Having a passion usually comes from seeing your career (work) as important and meaningful in a greater-than-self perspective, or purpose driven. Most businesses have the potential to contribute to the betterment of the human condition.

Successful leaders make the connection through vision, and then drive it by inspirational leadership into a culture that says, "Our/your contribution is important beyond just yourself," especially when the environment sees that you, as a *Valued Partner™*, are important in the process of adding value to "the greater good" served through your business. This, in addition to creating a positive collaborative environment that reduces communication obstacles, will foster the emotion of Passion for the work and the business.

When a company has passionate team members, there is a palpable air of success that is naturally transferred into the product and the customers. The passion for "your" business is Passed On to others more effectively. As your team understands and acts upon its power in the company, you have more success with customers.

Don't you just love it when you are in a business that exudes passion! It is contagious and it gets passed on to everyone inside and outside the business. It "works" as a positive and powerful loop of re-infection—the kind of epidemic every business wants, yet seldom has to insure success on all levels.

Wright

How do you coach business leaders to create passion?

Daugherty

Every successful business leader wants to work in an environment where passion abounds. Passion in the business is like a shot of adrenalin and is the antidote for being average or below average. Passion is the antidote that can solve the same ole' issues in the workplace. The hope of that being a possible reality leads many to pursue the fundamental four in a serious way.

The Fundamental Four™ is the jet fuel for creating and sustaining a world-class business. The discipline of the *Fundamental Four™* process is a good way to initiate great success. It requires leadership focus, which leads to discovering what is important to you as a vision. The leadership driven establishment of the business culture and *Valued Partners™* advanced skill sets will create passion within the team. Tie the vision to the bigger-than-us reason it is important, with some greater good for humanity, and that makes it even more important.

Example: When I was an orthodontist, my vision was to "change the world one smile at a time." We all knew that our efforts were going to first change the lives of our patients, which would add to the success and accomplishments of our patients' lives. This affects the world as a whole in some form, which made us co-contributors to the global initiative. All of us saw our job as more important than just applying braces, scheduling appointments, or filing insurance. We were making an impact on real people and the world, one patient at a time. We came to work with a purpose and that created passion for the day's work. That motivated us to constantly improve our knowledge and skills. When we left work each day we did so with the feeling that we produced something worthwhile and important beyond the paycheck we received.

Passion is important and is ignited and fanned by the *Fundamental Four™* disciplines. Keep in mind that the *Fundamental Four™* is the foundation upon which the other simple business success principals are constructed. These include the following business success systems:

- Simple Management Process—Valued Partner Success System
- Simple Technical Systems—The Innovate and Re-Invent Process
- Simple People Management Systems—Leader Success Systems
- Simple Business Growth Systems and The Relational Marketing Cookbooks

Wright

You have a lot of enthusiasm around your term *Valued Partners*™. Drill a little deeper in this area for us.

Daugherty

A *Valued Partner*™ is a high level knowledgeable worker who is engaged and passionate about the work and business—a real valuable asset in any business and your dream team member personified. Part of the vision and culture you create has to do with what your people would do and how they would behave if each of them were an ideal team member—a *Valued Partner*™—in your business.

As the leader, just as it is with your business vision, you must convey the message verbally to the team. Most business leaders tend to just assume that their team knows what the leaders envision the business to be or their ideal role in the business. They must know clearly and crisply how *you—the business leader*—sees it in detail! How? By your telling them how they fit into the picture. They need to know your version of what the ideal team member does and how each one of them contributes and succeeds in your business. They need to know what you expect and why it is important to the success of the business. Let them know how to become a success in your eyes and how to collaborate with each other to improve the entire business.

I recommend the Teach, Train, Trust approach with *Valued Partners*™ process. The process of success here involves appealing to key basic human needs such as certainty, significance, belonging, growth, and contribution, all of which are tied to being a *Valued Partner*™.

I believe few people in the world really want to just come to work and punch in, punch out, and go home. They really want to come to work feeling valuable and valued. We all want to feel that what we are doing is tied to something noble and worthwhile. As leaders we need to see what is noble in what we are doing and translate that into our business culture. Then let our employees run with it and make their noble business as great as it can be.

Wright

I understand you have developed a process to elevate employees into *Valued Partners*™ in business.

Daugherty

Yes, the system de-mystifies the process and engages team members in a way that a high percent will aspire to be *Valued Partners*™

in the company. I think every leader sees *Valued Partners*™ as important. It is similar to the process for business leaders, yet geared toward the team members that you want and need to drive the business. Due to shear numbers and "points of contact" the team drives the business anyway, for better or worse. How successful is your team's driving record? The system causes them to look at their vision and their "family business," how they lead that business in the business world, and then how they interact with others to create more success for the team and the company—everyone wins!

When an employee ties his or her personal success in your company to his or her own "family business" (family support reasons for having a job), it has new meaning. This gives purpose to becoming better and succeeding, along with job satisfaction and striving to be a *Valued Partner*™ on the team.

We assist *Valued Partners*™ in looking for ways that they can collaborate and make the company better without any "push" from management. *Valued Partners*™ help each other grow in each one's field of influence, "manage up," and synergistically move the company forward successfully. This reduces and/or avoids explosions in the "mine field" of office politics and communication nightmares.

Wright

What other areas do you teach in your speaking and consulting business?

Daugherty

I speak on personal and business success in several areas for general business and practices. I train teams on improving client or customer services. I work with growth strategies, team driven relational marketing strategies, and implementation systems. These are simple systems that insure powerful, positive, consistent, and repeatable results every time, with no exceptions!

I have created numerous programs. Some listed are processes for business and success enhancement:
- Five Simple Steps that Guarantee Business Success
- The Six Disciplines of Simplifying Business Success
- The Five Simple Keys to Creating a World-class Business
- Turning Single Customers into a Referral Machines
- Turning Ordinary Teams into *Valued Partners*™
- The Six Keys to Creating a World-class Practice
- The Practice Success System

- The Practice Marketing Matrix
- You can become a World-class Company

Wright

What a great conversation. I've learned a lot here today. I really appreciate all this time you've taken with me to answer these questions. I'm sure our readers are going to learn a lot.

Daugherty

David, thank you very much. It's been my pleasure.

About the Author

DR. TERRY DAUGHERTY was a highly respected orthodontist and business entrepreneur in the Dallas area. Developing a world-class practice that combined technical, people, and business excellence, he created a system for multiplying the concept in other practices through his simple systems and processes.

He is a National Speakers Association member, author, coach, consultant, and inspiring speaker for various companies nationwide. The principles of business success process, growth strategies, unparalleled service, relational psychology, and inspirational leadership are the core elements of his message.

Dr. Daugherty assists business leaders in getting the most out of their business, their teams, and themselves. Additionally, he helps team (staff) members become Valued Partners™ so they can get the most out of their careers, focusing on a high result, low stress approach.

Dr. Terry Daugherty
21 Hanover Way, Bluffton
South Carolina 29910
Phone: 843.837.7770
E-mail: Terry@DaughertyConsulting.com
www.DaughertyConsulting.com

Chapter 8

MATTHEW BEST

THE INTERVIEW

David Wright (Wright)

Matthew Best is an Entrepreneurial Coach and President of *Best Solutions.* Matthew focuses a great deal of his work with people who suffer from EADD, Entrepreneurial Attention Deficit Disorder—a term he coined to describe the "symptoms" many of his clients suffer from. Matthew finds that the biggest challenges most entrepreneurs and commission-based salespeople face are being able to focus, stay on message, and develop the most effective attitudes to accomplish their goals.

Matthew welcome to *Speaking of Success.*

Matthew Best (Best)

Thank you very much.

Wright

You have a unique and creative brand—Someday Isle. Would you explain the concept?

Best

It's a question that I typically love to ask people when I meet them and they ask me what I do. The question I always ask is, "Have you ever heard of a place called *Someday Isle?*" And of course half the people get it and half the people don't. It's the idea that *someday I'll do this; someday I'll do that.* I take my clients to *Someday Isle* the way I love to tell people about it.

What I found is that a lot of people love to talk big but there are few people who are willing to actually do the actions necessary to help them accomplish their goal and their dreams. The brand that I have really takes that head on.

Ultimately it also deals with time because so often people have this idea of what they want to accomplish and the timeframe that goes with it. They don't have a good understanding of the past, present, and future. It is ultimately about being focused about where you are right now. That's really what *Someday Isle* is all about.

Wright

And you describe yourself as an Entrepreneurial Coach. What's that?

Best

It's a term one of my colleagues used to describe himself and I felt that it fit perfectly with the type of folks I work with. I work with people who have an entrepreneurial spirit about them. They're either business owners, people in sales, or decision-makers within businesses.

I have a unique background when it comes to coaching. Most people have a background in corporate America and I don't. I have a background in politics. I've also had my own business in the past as well as having my own business now, so I'm an entrepreneur. Entrepreneur coaches really *focus* on a specific group of people—people who are entrepreneurs in nature. Entrepreneurs are a different breed of people.

I was talking to somebody today about entrepreneurism and we had a great connection. We have the willingness to take a challenge, take a risk, and really meet things head on. That's really what being an Entrepreneur Coach is. When I'm dealing with my clients, it's focusing on EADD as you mentioned in the beginning.

Wright

Interesting, what's EADD?

Best

It's a term I coined to describe what a lot of my clients suffer from when they first start working with me. It's actually something that I came up with because I was suffering from it. Obviously it is easy for me to identify it when I see it.

EADD stands for: Entrepreneurial Attention Deficit Disorder. The best way to describe it is to describe the characteristics of people who suffer from EADD. Who are these people? I have a full list on my Web site at: somedayisland.com, so I'll just name a few of them. Usually they are small or medium-sized business owners. They are people who work on a commission basis. They are people who have a million things to accomplish all at once. They are very driven people. They are people who want to accomplish things, who want to get a lot of things done, and who are willing to work long hours. They love and thrive on a challenge. They are risk-takers.

Those are people who are more likely to suffer from EADD. The problem is that EADD can cause so many different things. Ultimately EADD is a lack of focus. People can have a great attitude as far as their job or their business but they just don't have the focus about the direction they're headed. They just want to accomplish it all and conquer the world, but they don't know in what direction to go. They don't know what they can be satisfied with right now; but they know they are going to find a way to succeed.

Wright

How do you help your clients overcome EADD?

Best

That's a great question. As I mentioned, EADD sufferers are very driven and busy people. But you've got to take that into consideration—they don't have time for messing around, they typically want to get right to the bottom line of things. The big thing with EADD is like anything else, they have to slow down.

Take the example of weight. If somebody weighs 250 pounds it took that person a very long time to get to that point. Overweight people have to recognize it's going to take a while to lose that weight. It's the same thing with EADD as well.

There are two things I focus with them on: First is attitude. Second is goal planning, which goes with the idea of focus.

Attitude is our habit of thought. It is our subconscious nature. It controls almost 90 percent of what we do every day. It's as simple as getting up and seeing that it's raining and saying, "It's a rainy Monday again; it's going to be a horrible day." You're going to end up doing the things you need to do just to find out that hey, you're right, you had a horrible day.

Goal planning is the idea of focus. So many people have a million things they want to accomplish. Number one, they often don't write them down, and if they do write them down they don't have a plan on how to get there. They don't know exactly what it is they need to do to accomplish that goal. When I ask people about their daily "To-do list" most people have thirty to fifty things on the list. That is just a lack of focus ultimately. They are trying to accomplish way too much and there is no way they can accomplish all those things in one day—they are setting themselves up for failure.

Getting people to be more focused is really about asking what they are spending their time doing. Are they spending their time on things that are going to help them accomplish their goal or are they spending their time on things that are just busy-work? There is a huge difference in being busy and being productive.

Wright

Since this is a book on success, Matthew, please share how you define success.

Best

I use the definition that a company I am affiliated with—"Resource Associates Corporation"—uses. They came up with this definition and I absolutely love it. I'll give you the definition and explain it a little bit. It is the continuous achievement of predetermined goals stabilized by balance and purified by belief.

What that means is that success is a journey and not a destination. The continuous achievement is just that—continual. You're always moving forward. It's as if you drive along in your car and you take note of the mile markers. You know that if you start at mile 100 and you're going to mile 250, when you pass mile marker 150 you know that you only have 100 more miles to go. Making predetermined goals means you are setting out exactly what you are going to accomplish, whether it's a personal or a business goal. It's determining ahead of time what the destination is going to be.

Stabilized by balance is really the whole idea that there are a million things out there that keep us from the whole idea of focus. People often focus so much on their financial success that other areas of their life—other areas of their business—can suffer. Success has to be well rounded. It can't be measured just financially because people can have all the money in the world but if they are not happy at home, if their health is suffering, if they're not expanding their mind, if they're losing their friends, is that really success? Success is achieving balance.

And lastly, the phrase "purified by belief" strikes to the heart of the whole idea of attitude. In going back to the example I just used, if people are financially successful but they don't believe in what they're doing, is that really success? One type of person I like to work with is people who are in sales. It's not even the sales development or sales training that I enjoy most. The reason I love working with salespeople is because the first element that anybody buys is the salesperson. So salespeople have to start off with a belief in themselves. They have to start off with a belief in their product to the point where they use their product for themselves. It's very much about their belief. Purified by belief is a very important part of that definition of success.

Wright

That's a great definition and explanation. How do people use that in a daily application?

Best

That's a great question. When it comes to the bottom line, that's what most people care about. It goes back to attitude and goal planning. You have to know where you're going and you've got to know why you're going there. The way I define leadership is: knowing who you are, where you are going, and who's coming along for the ride. That's really what success is about. It is self-leadership and formal leadership.

I talk about attitude, which is another key ingredient to the daily application. Some of that has to do with the self-talk we have within ourselves—that whole idea that today is a rainy Monday or if people have a messy office. If they believe they have a messy office they will do what they do to have a messy office and then they'll be absolutely right.

Our attitude drives our behavior, which drives our results. Our behavior cannot contradict our attitude on a consistent basis. What's going on inside of our own mind is very important and it affects so much of what happens and so much of our success. The attitude is taking a look at and being aware of what is going on inside of my mind right now. It's being aware of the big picture, that goal. What's that goal I'm trying to accomplish? Why do I want to accomplish it? What are the right attitudes that I have to have—the right thoughts?

The other element that is a part of the daily application is making goals. Goals are really nothing more than focus—focusing on what's important. If you're doing something that is not related to your goal, then you have to ask yourself why you are doing it. Every single day it's starting off with a plan for that day. People may have a plan for a week, but often, if they are just getting started, it's planning out that day and figuring out what can be accomplished that day realistically without going too far and without planning too much. Ask what things must be done *today* that will help accomplish the goal. There is that old adage, "Rome wasn't built in a day." The same thing is true with goals. You can't accomplish it all in one day. An entire shopping mall can't be built in one day. It takes years to build a mall. Why would it be any different for us in accomplishing our goals?

The fourth thing that I mentioned in *Daily Application* would be letting go. This also relates to time management. I have a saying in relation to time management: "Managing time is like raking water—it can't be done." I have a colleague who says that time management problems are not about time; they are about goal clarification issues. The more we understand about where we are headed, the more success we'll have. On a daily basis start by looking at how much you have scheduled to do.

The last thing is the schedule, of course. Most people schedule way too many things, as I mentioned before. Ask, "What am I capable of doing today?" And then don't schedule too much more. Schedule other tasks for the future. There's no reason that everything must happen today if it doesn't have to.

Wright

Would you tell me what you mean by attitude?

Best

That's another great question. Attitude, as I mentioned very briefly, is the habit of thought. Attitude is that subconscious nature—what we are thinking about and what our beliefs are about a situation, what we're pursuing, our experiences, and our expectations. We get exactly what we expect to happen.

A great example is when you think of people in sales who have the fear of picking up the phone and calling somebody, especially making a cold call. Cold calls are a great example. People will get ready and then they'll make excuses about why they're not picking up the phone and making the calls. Ultimately, what's going on in their mind is the idea that they don't want to be a telemarketer. No one likes it. I don't like it when a telemarketer calls me, so I don't want to be a telemarketer. It's the same concept.

An example is a client I have. One of the things we worked on is his messy office. I asked him what he had done in the past about his messy office. He said that his wife came in, held up every single piece of paper, and said, "What are you going to do with it?" It was either delegate it or dump it.

I asked him how it worked out. He said that it was fine and it was cleaned up. I then asked him how long it stayed clean and he told me that it lasted about two weeks, then it was back to the way it was.

"Well all right," I said, "what I want you to do is to start thinking differently. I need you to start believing that you have a clean office and I don't want you to do anything else."

So I worked with him on attitude and a little bit of affirmation and what a clean office meant to him. After a couple of weeks I specifically ask him a question about his office and he said that he had been avoiding the office. I told him that he was doing great, keep going at it. He looked at me strangely. I just reaffirmed to him to keep going, he was fine. A couple of weeks later (actually a little longer than that) again I asked him about his office.

"You won't believe this," he said, "but the office is clean and it's been clean for weeks now."

"What happened?" I asked.

"I finally got to the point where I got so sick of it I cleaned it and I cleaned it to the point where it became the picture I had in my mind of it."

I would almost guarantee that if I went back to him right now, that office is still clean just because of the simple fact that his attitude affected his behavior and he got the result he wanted. That's ultimately what attitude is all about.

Wright

Would you also share what it means to do effective goal-planning?

Best

Effective goal-planning is a great concept. The whole point of planning out goals is to have focus so that we know what it is we're going

going to do. We know how we're going to do it and the specific actions we will take to accomplish it.

There's a concept that another colleague (one of my coaches), David Herdlinger, taught me. It is the concept stated in an acronym: WHY SMART. A lot of people have heard about smart goals but very few people have heard about WHY SMART goals. I'm going to share that:

W—Stands for *Written*. Having written goals is so very important. When you write something down you are seeing it twice because you're thinking about it and then you're also seeing it on paper. The other benefit of writing something down is that it gets it out of your mind. That in of itself is helping you get some focus. You have pure thoughts going on in your mind.

I've seen studies before where a group of people were asked to make a resolution. One third of the group was asked to make the resolution. Six months later they were asked how it was going and very few people had accomplished or kept doing what they had resolved at the beginning of the year.

The same concept was applied to the next group except they were told to write their resolutions down and then tuck them away. Six months later a small percentage had kept their resolutions but a larger percentage had kept their resolutions than those who had not written anything down.

The last group wrote their resolutions down and were told to look at their resolutions every single week. And of course, six months later those were the folks who were more focused—they were more successful than any of the other groups by far. A larger percentage of those people kept their resolutions. So that is the power of writing things down.

H—Stands for *Harmonious*, which means that the goal must fit in with everything else that's going on. If you think of businesses that have Vision Statements, they will also have Mission Statements and they will have Value Statements. Ask if the goal fits in with those—the vision, the mission, and the values—or is the goal something that just doesn't make sense?

A great example that I saw once was an ad in the paper. The ad was for a toy store that also sold guns. I wondered what was going on there. That didn't really make sense. Harmonious is just making sure everything is aligned.

Y—Is *Yours*, which is very important when you are setting goals. The goals must have some sort of personal meaning for you. It's got to have some sort of personal reward and some kind of personal consequence if you don't accomplish it, otherwise there won't be enough meaning in it to motivate you.

It's really important to identify the motivation. Why do you want to accomplish this goal? Is it something that your boss said that indicated you really need to accomplish this? Frankly, you will not do it very well unless there is some kind of personal motivation behind it. You can get that even in a business. If somebody's personal goals are aligned with their professional and business goals, that person's going to be right on target.

S—Stands for *Specific*. Something has to be specific so that you can see the end result before you even get there. There are so many times when I'm working with my clients and I discover that being specific is the hardest thing for them to do—what will the end result actually look like? So many people have an easy time identifying what they *don't* want, but they have a tough time identifying what it is that they *do* want. So being specific really means getting that picture of what is it that you want in a personal sense. If it's that black BMW sitting in the lot somewhere that you drive by and you think, "That is my BMW and I'm going to have that some day;" it's taking a picture of that car so you can see it all the time. You know exactly what it looks like. That's what being specific is.

M—Stands for *Measurable*. This is really important because if you can measure something, you can accomplish it. That is the simple version of what measuring is. If you are making phone calls, how many phone calls do you need to do to accomplish your result? As you're making phone calls you can just check it off—it's measurable. That's the simple version of *Measurable*.

A—Is *Attainable*. Attainable means it is within your capacity and your capabilities to accomplish this goal. This really gets to the difference between a dream and a goal. Dreams are something you think about. Goals are something that you act upon. You can only act on the thing(s) you are capable of acting on.

One of my coaches had a dream to be an NBA all-star. The problem is that he's in his fifties and he weighs 250 pounds. It's never going to happen. It's not attainable and he recognizes that, so it's on his dream list and that's okay. He knows that it's not an attainable goal for him.

It's taking a look at the current resources you have and then asking yourself if it is possible to accomplish this goal?

R—Is *Realistically High.* This is behind the whole idea of stretching yourself. People love using the concept of low hanging fruit in trees when they are dealing with sales. It's not the low hanging fruit we're talking about here. *Realistically High* means that the goal you want to reach is at the top level of the tree and you want to get the apples up there. You might not reach the top level but you're going to reach a lot higher up and get the better fruit that's higher than the low hanging fruit. That's ultimately what *Realistically High* is—it's shooting for the stars and getting into space. Who knows—you might actually reach the stars.

T—Has to do with *Time Bound.* There has got to be some kind of timetable to your goal. Otherwise you can keep putting it off until tomorrow. Time is nothing more than a goal clarification issue. Time is such an important thing because it is measurable. You can see how many days you have left in the month, in the quarter, in the year. That's actually a two-for-one thing—you get something that's measurable and you get time when you're dealing with time.

When I'm talking about effective goal-planning I'm really talking about WHY SMART.

Wright

Would you tell our readers a little bit about what drives you to succeed?

Best

I coined the term EADD. I've suffered from it and I know what it's like. I love a challenge. I'm a very driven individual. My background is in politics, which is a very challenging arena. I took a look at the whole idea of success a while back and I looked at what it was that I really enjoyed and why I enjoyed those things.

Being involved in campaign politics is all about the thrill of victory and the agony of defeat. It's a challenge, especially when you're working with challengers to incumbents.

I love running marathons. Again it's a challenge—it's a personal challenge. Can I take my body 26.2 miles after having trained three to four months?

Owning my own business is a challenge because I have no one else to be accountable to. It's a challenge every single day. Ultimately what drives me is that challenge.

I came up with a purpose statement for myself a while back and the purpose statement very simply says, "I exist to serve by unleashing courage." And that's really what drives me. When I take a look at that phrase, the picture that comes to my mind is the picture of a dog on a leash. The dog is restricted in how far he can go because he's on the leash. The words came to me: "unleashing courage." It was the idea of a hand reaching out and taking off that leash; now the dog is free. He can go or he can stay mentally attached to the leash. That's really what drives me—saying that I can help you by unleashing you; but it's up to you as far as where you want to go. It's true for me. It's true for my clients and anybody else I work with.

Wright

What is the message you want people to hear so they can learn from your success?

Best

I recently heard a great quote just in the last week. It was absolutely perfect: "After you get tired you can still go a long way." I don't know who said it but the statement is so true and it's true in politics, it's true in marathon running, it's true in having your own business, it's true in sales, and it's true in so many areas of life.

The big concept behind it is the idea of persistence. It's the difference, I believe, between people who are committed to success and those who are only interested in success. Those who are not committed usually end up giving up. It takes a lot of courage to keep going when you're tired, when you're hurting financially, physically, and in other ways. It takes a lot of courage to let go of always having to be in control of everything. It takes courage to succeed.

That's the big message—have courage and be persistent because it's a price worth paying and the rewards are great.

Wright

What a great conversation, Matthew. I really appreciate your taking all this time with me today to answer all these questions. You've given me a lot to think about and you've given a lot of information to our readers.

Best

Thank you so much. I know I've had a great time.

About the Author

MATTHEW BEST is an Entrepreneurial Coach dedicated to working with his clients to cure EADD—Entrepreneurial Attention Deficit Disorder—a phrase he coined to describe the "symptoms" his clients suffer from before they work with him.

Matthew graduated with a degree in Political Science from Grove City College. He then went to Washington, D.C., where he worked for a U.S. Congressman and then for a lobbyist. Upon moving to Carlisle, Pennsylvania, he started a government affairs firm. He then worked for a state representative. During all of this time, Matthew has also been involved in campaign politics and managing political campaigns at various levels of government. These experiences have given Matthew a unique perspective on the importance of attitude development and goal clarification. He puts that perspective to good use with his clients in their efforts to be successful.

Matthew is a published author of several articles appearing in regional and national publications. He is an avid marathon runner, and of course, he loves a challenge.

Matthew Best
Best Solutions
5 Ascot Lane
Carlisle, PA 17013
Phone: 717.557.5001
E-mail: matt@somedayisland.com
www.somedayisland.com

Chapter 9

DR. STEPHEN R. COVEY

David Wright (Wright)

We're talking today with Dr. Stephen R. Covey, cofounder and vice-chairman of Franklin Covey Company, the largest management company and leadership development organization in the world. Dr. Covey is perhaps best known as the author of *The 7 Habits of Highly Effective People* which is ranked as a number one best seller by the *New York Times*, having sold more than fourteen million copies in thirty-eight languages throughout the world. Dr. Covey is an internationally respected leadership authority, family expert, teacher, and organizational consultant. He has made teaching principle-centered living and principle-centered leadership his life's work. Dr. Covey is the recipient of the Thomas More College Medallion for Continuing Service to Humanity and has been awarded four honorary doctorate degrees. Other awards given Dr. Covey include the Sikh's 1989 International Man of Peace award, the 1994 International Entrepreneur of the Year award, *Inc.* magazine's Services Entrepreneur of the Year award, and in 1996 the National Entrepreneur of the Year Lifetime Achievement award for Entrepreneurial leadership. He has also been recognized as one of *Time* magazine's twenty-five most influential Americans and one of Sales and Marketing Management's top twenty-five power brokers. Dr. Covey earned his undergraduate degree from the University of Utah, his MBA from Harvard, and completed his doctorate at Brigham Young University. While at Brigham Young he served as assistant to the President and was also a professor of business management and organizational behavior.

Dr. Covey, welcome to *Speaking of Success!*

Dr. Stephen Covey (Covey)

Thank you.

Wright

Dr. Covey, most companies make decisions and filter them down through their organization. You, however, state that no company can succeed until individuals within it succeed. Are the goals of the company the result of the combined goals of the individuals?

Covey

Absolutely, because if people aren't on the same page, they're going to be pulling in different directions. To teach this concept, I frequently ask large audiences to close their eyes and point north, and then to keep pointing and open their eyes and they find themselves pointing all over the place. I say to them, "Tomorrow morning if you want a similar experience, ask the first ten people you meet in your organization what the purpose of your organization is and you'll find it's a very similar experience. They'll point all over the place." When people have a different sense of purpose and values, every decision that is made from then on is governed by those. There's no question that this is one of the fundamental causes of misalignment, low trust, interpersonal conflict, interdepartmental rivalry, people operating on personal agendas, and so forth.

Wright

Is that mostly a result of the inability to communicate from the top?

Covey

That's one aspect, but I think it's more fundamental. There's an inability to involve people—an unwillingness. Leaders may communicate what their mission and their strategy is, but that doesn't mean there's any emotional connection to it. Mission statements that are rushed and then announced are soon forgotten. They become nothing more than just a bunch of platitudes on the wall that mean essentially nothing and even create a source of cynicism and a sense of hypocrisy inside the culture of an organization.

Wright

How do companies ensure survival and prosperity in these tumultuous times of technological advances, mergers, downsizing, and change?

Covey

I think that it takes a lot of high trust in a culture that has something that doesn't change—principles—at its core. There are principles that people agree upon that are valued. It gives a sense of stability. Then you have the power to adapt and be flexible when you experience these kinds of disruptive new economic models or technologies that come in and sideswipe you. You don't know how to handle them unless you have something you can depend upon. If people have not agreed to a common set of principles that guide them and a common purpose, then they get their security from the outside and they tend to freeze the structure, systems, and processes inside and they cease becoming adaptable. They don't change with the changing realities of the new marketplace out there and gradually they become obsolete.

Wright

I was interested in one portion of your book *The 7 Habits of Highly Effective People* where you talk about behaviors. How does an individual go about the process of replacing ineffective behaviors with effective ones?

Covey

I think that for most people it usually requires a crisis that humbles them to become aware of their ineffective behaviors. If there's not a crisis the tendency is to perpetuate those behaviors and not change. You don't have to wait until the marketplace creates the crisis for you. Have everyone accountable on a 360 degree basis to everyone else they interact with—with feedback either formal or informal—where they are getting data as to what's happening. They will then start to realize that the consequences of their ineffective behavior require them to be humble enough to look at that behavior and to adopt new, more effective ways of doing things. Sometimes people can be stirred up to this if you just appeal to their conscience—to their inward sense of what is right and wrong. A lot of people sometimes know inwardly they're doing wrong, but the culture doesn't necessarily discourage them from continuing that. They either need feedback from people, or they need feedback from the marketplace, or they need feedback from their conscience. Then they can begin to develop a step-by-step process of replacing old habits with new, better habits.

Wright

It's almost like saying, "Let's make all the mistakes in the laboratory before we put this thing in the air."

Covey

Right; and I also think what is necessary is a paradigm shift, which is analogous to having a correct map, say of a city or of a country. If people have an inaccurate paradigm of life, of other people, and of themselves it really doesn't make much difference what their behavior or habits or attitudes are. What they need is a correct paradigm—a correct map—that describes what's going on. For instance, in the Middle Ages they used to heal people through bloodletting. It wasn't until Samuel Weiss and Pasteur and other empirical scientists discovered the germ theory that they realized for the first time they weren't dealing with the real issue. They realized why women preferred to use midwives who washed rather than doctors who didn't wash. They gradually got a new paradigm. Once you've got a new paradigm then your behavior and your attitude flows directly from it. If you have a bad paradigm or a bad map, let's say of a city, there's no way, no matter what your behavior or your habits or your attitudes are—how positive they are—you'll never be able to find the location you're looking for. This is why I believe that to change paradigms is far more fundamental than to work on attitude and behavior.

Wright

One of your seven habits of highly effective people is to begin with the end in mind. If circumstances change and hardships or miscalculation occurs, how does one view the end with clarity?

Covey

Many people think to begin with the end in mind means that you have some fixed definition of a goal that's accomplished and if changes come about you're not going to adapt to them. Instead, the "end in mind" you begin with is that you are going to create a flexible culture of high trust so that no matter what comes along you are going to do whatever it takes to accommodate that new change or that new reality and maintain a culture of high performance and high trust. You're talking more in terms of values and overall purposes that don't change, rather than specific strategies or programs that will have to change to accommodate the changing realities in the marketplace.

Wright

In this time of mistrust between people, corporations, and nations for that matter, how do we create high levels of trust?

Covey

That's a great question and it's complicated because there are so many elements that go into the creating of a culture of trust. Obviously the most fundamental one is just to have trustworthy people. But that is not sufficient because what if the organization itself is misaligned? For instance, what if you say you value cooperation but you really reward people for internal competition? Then you have a systemic or a structure problem that creates low trust inside the culture even though the people themselves are trustworthy. This is one of the insights of Edward Demming and the work he did. That's why he said that most problems are not personal; they're systemic. They're common caused. That's why you have to work on structure, systems, and processes to make sure that they institutionalize principle-centered values. Otherwise you could have good people with bad systems and you'll get bad results.

When it comes to developing interpersonal trust between people, it is made up of many, many elements such as taking the time to listen to other people, to understand them, and to see what is important to them. What we think is important to another may only be important to us, not to another. It takes empathy. You have to make and keep promises to them. You have to treat them with kindness and courtesy. You have to be completely honest and open. You have to live up to your commitments. You can't betray them behind their back. You can't badmouth them behind their back and sweet-talk them to their face. That will send out vibes of hypocrisy and it will be detected. You have to learn to apologize when you make mistakes, to admit mistakes, and to also get feedback going in every direction as much as possible. It doesn't necessarily require formal forums; it requires trust between people that will be open with each other and give each other feedback.

Wright

My mother told me to do a lot of what you're saying now, but it seems like when I got in business I simply forgot.

Covey

Sometimes we forget, but sometimes culture doesn't nurture it. That's why I say unless you work with the institutionalizing—that means formalizing into structure, systems, and processes the values—you will not have a nurturing culture. You have to constantly work on that. This is one of the big mistakes organizations make. They think trust is simply a function of being honest. That's only one small aspect. It's an important aspect, obviously, but there are so many other elements that go into the creation of a high trust culture.

Wright

"Seek first to understand then to be understood" is another of your seven habits. Do you find that people try to communicate without really understanding what other people want?

Covey

Absolutely. The tendency is to project out of our own autobiography—our own life, our own value system—onto other people, thinking we know what they want. So we don't really listen to them. We pretend to listen, but we really don't listen from within their frame of reference. We listen from within our own frame of reference and we're really preparing our reply rather than seeking to understand. This is a very common thing. In fact very few people have had any training in seriously listening. They're trained in how to read, write, and speak, but not to listen.

Reading, writing, speaking, and listening are the four modes of communication and they represent about two-thirds to three-fourths of our waking hours. About half of that time is spent listening, but it's the one skill people have not been trained in. People have had all this training in the other forms of communication. In a large audience of

1,000 people you wouldn't have more than twenty people who have had more than two weeks of training in listening. Listening is more than a skill or a technique so that you're listening within another frame of reference. It takes tremendous courage to listen because you're at risk when you listen. You don't know what's going to happen; you're vulnerable.

Wright

Sales gurus always tell me that the number one skill in selling is listening.

Covey

Yes—listening from within the customer's frame of reference. That is so true. You can see that it takes some security to do that because you don't know what's going to happen.

Wright

With our *Speaking of Success!* talk show and book we're trying to encourage people in our audience to be better, to live better, and be more fulfilled by listening to the examples of our guests. Is there anything or anyone in your life that has made a difference for you and helped you to become a better person?

Covey

I think the most influential people in my life have been my parents. I think that what they modeled was not to make comparisons and harbor jealousy or to seek recognition. They were humble people. I remember my mother one time when we were going up in an elevator and the most prominent person in the state was in the elevator. She knew him, but she spent her time talking to the elevator operator. I was just a little kid and I was so awed by this person and I said to my mom, "Why didn't you talk to the important person?" She said, "I was. I had never met him." They were really humble, modest people who were focused on service and other people rather than on themselves. I think they were very inspiring models to me.

Wright

In almost every research paper that anyone I've ever read writes about people who influenced their lives, in the top five people, three of them are teachers. My seventh grade English teacher was the greatest teacher I ever had and influenced me to no end.

Covey

Would it be correct to say that she saw in you probably some qualities of greatness you didn't even see in yourself?

Wright

Absolutely.

Covey

That's been my general experience that the key aspect of a mentor or a teacher is someone who sees in you potential that you don't even see in yourself. They treat you accordingly and eventually you come to see it in yourself. That's my definition of leadership or influence—communicating people's worth and potential so clearly that they are inspired to see it in themselves.

Wright

Most of my teachers treated me as a student, but she treated me with much more respect than that. As a matter of fact, she called me Mr. Wright in the seventh grade. I'd never been addressed by anything but a nickname. I stood a little taller; she just made a tremendous difference. Do you think there are other characteristics that mentors seem to have in common?

Covey

I think they are first of all good examples in their own personal lives. Their personal lives and their family lives are not all messed up—they come from a base of good character. They also are usually very confident and they take the time to do what your teacher did to you—to treat you with uncommon respect and courtesy.

They also, I think, explicitly teach principles rather than practices so that rules don't take the place of human judgment. You gradually come to have faith in your own judgment in making decisions because of the affirmation of such a mentor. Good mentors care about you— you can feel the sincerity of their caring. It's like the expression, "I don't care how much you know until I know how much you care."

Wright

Most people are fascinated with the new television shows about being a survivor. What has been the greatest comeback that you've made from adversity in your career or your life?

Covey

When I was in grade school I experienced a disease in my legs. It caused me to use crutches for a while. I tried to get off them fast and get back. The disease wasn't corrected yet so I went back on crutches for another year. The disease went to the other leg and I went on for another year. It essentially took me out of my favorite thing—athletics—and it took me more into being a student. So that was kind of a life-defining experience which at the time seemed very negative, but has proven to be the basis on which I've focused my life—being more of a learner.

Wright

Principle-centered learning is basically what you do that's different from anybody I've read or listened to.

Covey

The concept is embodied in the far-eastern expression, "Give a man a fish, you feed him for the day; teach him how to fish, you feed him for a lifetime." When you teach principles that are universal and timeless, they don't belong to just any one person's religion or to a particular culture or geography. They seem to be timeless and universal like the ones we've been talking about here: trustworthiness, honesty, caring, service, growth, and development. These are universal principles. If you focus on these things then little by little people become independent of you and then they start to believe in themselves and their own judgment becomes better. You don't need as many rules. You don't need as much bureaucracy and as many controls and you can empower people.

The problem in most business operations today—and not just business but non-business—is that they're using the industrial model in an information age. Arnold Toynbee, the great historian, said, "You can pretty well summarize all of history in four words: nothing fails like success." The industrial model was based on the asset of the machine. The information model is based on the asset of the person—the knowledge worker. It's an altogether different model. But the machine model was the main asset of the twentieth century. It enabled productivity to increase fifty times. The new asset is intellectual and social capital—the qualities of people and the quality of the relationship they have with each other. Like Toynbee said, "Nothing fails like success." The industrial model does not work in an information age. It requires a focus on the new wealth, not capital and material things.

A good illustration that demonstrates how much we were into the industrial model, and still are, is to notice where people are on the balance sheet. They're not found there. Machines are found there. Machines become investments. People are on the profit and loss statement and people are expenses. Think of that—if that isn't blood-letting.

Wright

It sure is.

When you consider the choices you've made down through the years, has faith played an important role in your life?

Covey

It has played an extremely important role. I believe deeply that we should put principles at the center of our lives, but I believe that God is the source of those principles. I did not invent them. I get credit sometimes for some of the Seven Habits material and some of the other things I've done, but it's really all based on principles that have been given by God to all of His children from the beginning of time. You'll find that you can teach these same principles from the sacred texts and the wisdom literature of almost any tradition. I think the ultimate source of that is God and that is one thing you can absolutely depend upon—in God we trust.

Wright

If you could have a platform and tell our audience something you feel would help them or encourage them, what would you say?

Covey

I think I would say to put God at the center of your life and then prioritize your family. No one on their deathbed ever wished they spent more time at the office.

Wright

That's right. We have come down to the end of our program and I know you're a busy person, but I could talk with you all day Dr. Covey.

Covey

It's good to talk with you as well and to be a part of this program. It looks like an excellent one that you've got going on here.

Wright

Thank you.

We have been talking today with Dr. Stephen R. Covey, co-founder and vice-chairman of Franklin Covey Company. He's also the author of *The 7 Habits of Highly Effective People,* which has been ranked as a number one bestseller by the *New York Times*, selling more than fourteen million copies in thirty-eight languages.

Dr. Covey, thank you so much for being with us today on *Speaking of Success!*

Covey

Thank you for the honor of participating.

About The Author

Stephen R. Covey was recognized in 1996 as one of Time magazine's twenty-five most influential Americans and one of Sales and Marketing Management's top twenty-five power brokers. Dr. Covey is the author of several acclaimed books, including the international bestseller, The 7 Habits of Highly Effective People. It has sold more than fifteen million copies in thirty-eight languages throughout the world. Other bestsellers authored by Dr. Covey include First Things First, Principle-Centered Leadership (with sales exceeding one million), and The 7 Habits of Highly Effective Families.

Dr. Covey's newest book, The 8th Habit: From Effectiveness to Greatness, which was released in November 2004, rose to the top of several bestseller lists, including New York Times, Wall Street Journal, USA Today, Money, Business Week, and Amazon.com and Barnes & Noble. The 8th Habit . . . has sold more than 360,000 copies.

Dr. Covey earned his undergraduate degree from the University of Utah, his MBA from Harvard, and completed his doctorate at Brigham Young University. While at Brigham Young University, he served as assistant to the President and was also a professor of business management and organizational behavior. He received the National Fatherhood Award in 2003, which, as the father of nine and grandfather of forty-four, he says is the most meaningful award he has ever received.

Dr. Covey currently serves on the board of directors for the Points of Light Foundation. Based in Washington, D.C., the Foundation, through its partnership with the Volunteer Center National Network, engages and mobilizes millions of volunteers from all walks of life—businesses, nonprofits, faith-based organizations, low-income communities, families, youth, and older adults—to help solve serious social problems in thousands of communities.

Dr. Stephen R. Covey
www.stephencovey.com

Chapter 10

LISA MARIE PLATSKE

David Wright (Wright)

Lisa Marie Platske, author of *Designing Your Destiny: Achieving Personal and Professional Success through Upside Thinking,* and co-author of the upcoming book, *Authentic Connections in Business,* is a dynamic motivational speaker, leadership coach, and consultant who founded Upside Thinking, Inc. to help others find more happiness, success, and meaning in their lives. She empowers audiences and clients with her upside thinking principles and cutting-edge leadership strategies to consider their possibilities, clarify their vision, and create positive change in their personal and professional lives.

Wright

What is "Upside Thinking"?

Lisa Marie Platske (Platske)

"Upside Thinking" is a philosophy combining three principles of excellence that are guaranteed to attract more happiness, success, and meaning into your life. It's a way of living and requires being intentional in everything you do, both personally and professionally. Those three principles of excellence are also what I refer to as core beliefs.

The first one is, "Everyone wants happiness, success, and meaning." We all have the same basic innate desires to achieve, thrive, and make a difference in this world; we just choose to accomplish these in different ways.

The second principle is, "Priorities have to be set up in the following order: Self and Health first, Family second, and Work third." If you don't take care of yourself first, you cannot properly give to your family or your work. And if you ignore the work/life balance, your self, family, and/or work will suffer.

The third principle of excellence is, "You are where you choose to be." We do, in fact, have the power to choose who we are and design our own destiny.

These all appear very simple, but it takes intentional effort to integrate them into our daily lives.

Wright

How is "Upside Thinking" different from positive thinking?

Platske

Every so often, someone will comment that "upside thinking must be just like positive thinking," but the definition of "upside" is not interchangeable with the word "positive." "Upside" means to see the unlimited possibilities in every circumstance.

My goal is to use "Upside Thinking" as a tool to empower others to make the best possible choices for their personal and professional lives. I use my life as an example by continually reviewing who I am, what I want, where I'm going, whether I like the direction that my life and company are headed, and why it matters because excellence is a journey, not a destination.

Wright

Do you get any opposition when you tell people to prioritize Self, Family, and then Work?

Platske

Yes, all the time. I find myself debating what I believe to be an important component of living a happy, successful, and meaningful life. The question is, "Why would I put myself first? And how can I possibly do that?" And my answer to this is always, "For the good of your self, your family, and your work; how can you not?"

Most of us have been taught since kindergarten to put others first. Consequently, I've met dozens of men and women who don't know what they want because they've always put the needs of the people around them before their own. Yet, if we are tired, stressed, and over-worked because we are not putting ourselves first, how can we be the best of who we are for our families and our businesses?

Wright

I remember the first time I flew on an airplane when I was a kid. The lady up front told us that when the oxygen masks fell down, you were supposed to put it on your face first and then give it to your child. I thought, "Are you an idiot or something?" It never occurred to me that if you don't take care of yourself, you sure couldn't take care of anybody else.

Platske

Exactly!

Wright

What is the focus of Upside Thinking, Inc.?

Platske

The focus—the mission—is to transform lives. That's the bottom line. Our goal is to help others determine what they want to do with their lives and achieve extraordinary results personally and professionally.

When I founded Upside Thinking, Inc., I was really determined to build an organization that would help others find this happiness, success, and meaning through individual development and understanding the power of possibility.

Upside Thinking, Inc. is an international leadership development company because I believe that leadership is the key to understanding the power of possibility. Our approach, however, is not just focused on business. It is a holistic one that incorporates body, mind, and spirit. Add the three core beliefs, throw in a little quantum physics, and you've got the secret formula for "Upside Thinking."

Wright

Everyone who hears you speak raves about your high energy and enthusiasm. Where does your energy come from?

Platske

My energy comes from living an Upside life. I live what I teach and look for the unlimited possibilities around me. And I do find them; I find them every day. I also believe I have a message that is worth hearing. Whether I'm in front of a group of 10 or 1,000, I'm hoping to change lives, not simply entertain.

As I said earlier, one of the core beliefs of Upside Thinking is, "You are where you choose to be," and I choose to be excited about life every moment of every day!

Wright

Lisa Marie, you're often heard speaking about work/life balance in your keynote speeches as well as in your motivational seminars. Why is this important to you?

Platske

When I started Upside Thinking, Inc., I spent a considerable amount of time determining what values would form the foundation of my new business venture. One of the three principles of excellence that you've heard me speak about several times in this interview is the prioritizing of your life—putting your Self first, your Family second, and your Work third. If you take care of your health and put yourself first, you can properly give the best of who you are to your family. If you have addressed all of the needs in your family, you can adequately give to your work. However, if you ignore that work/life balance, something is going to suffer, whether it's your self, your family, or your work.

We all get the same twenty-four-hour allotment per day. It doesn't make a difference how much money you make, what your family background is, or what your job or title is, it's the same for every one of us.

Long workdays and little or no vacation have become very common in the United States, and I believe that most Americans choose to live unbalanced lives. They think that their work is an investment in their future, figuring that they are going to retire earlier or reward themselves later. However, there is no guarantee that later will ever arrive. If it does, it might not be packaged the way that we envisioned, which is why it is important to treasure every moment and understand that it's a gift. That is why it's called the *present.*

Life is a balancing act, and I think it's very easy to get caught in the business of life—going from one activity to the next. I have to fight it myself. If we're not careful, success can come at the expense of something more valuable. I've watched it happen to several people in my life, and it is one of the biggest issues with all of my coaching clients.

Wright

What do you think are the biggest obstacles people face in trying to become successful in speaking or in any entrepreneurial venture?

Platske

Most people would say that the biggest obstacles are building credibility, lack of support from family and friends, finding a mentor, or even lack of capital. All of those challenges can be extremely difficult, but I believe they are minor compared to the challenge of believing in yourself. People fear success far more than they'll ever fear failure, and their self-imposed limitations prevent them from achieving greatness.

I believe that everyone is extraordinary, but because they see themselves as average, they never allow those unique and amazing qualities to shine. It's one thing to ask for something; it's a completely different set of emotions to believe that you're going to get it.

Wright

Is there something that serves as the catalyst for your success?

Platske

The Law of Attraction—like attracts like. When I believe something will happen, I believe it deep down in the core of my being. When I do that, it always happens. Always. I don't have any exceptions. I think it also has to do with one of the main reasons why I want to be successful: giving money and time (volunteerism) to increase the well-being of mankind is so important to me. The more I achieve and earn, the more I have to give.

Wright

Someone told me years ago that a definition of a great citizen is that person who puts more into the community than he or she takes out. Not bad.

Platske

I like that definition. I spent more than a decade in federal law enforcement, including work in Homeland Security, before I began Upside Thinking, Inc., and I really believe in the importance of doing what we can to make this world a better place. It takes people who are willing to serve the community with whatever resources they have—time for volunteerism, money for projects, or excellent leadership. It's disconcerting to think what would happen to our world if we kept all of these gifts to ourselves.

Wright

What is *Authentic Connections in Business?*

Platske

One of my closest friends and strategic business partners, Ursula Mentjes, and I would meet at one of our favorite restaurants, Table for Two. We would often discuss the elements of business that one needs to master in order to create a successful business, and one of the most important elements is making authentic connections. Ursula is a sales coach and a speaker, so we both work with executives, senior managers, and entrepreneurs who are looking for significant and long-lasting improvement in their personal and professional lives. In March of 2006, we decided that we would share our formula about what actually makes an *authentic connection* happen and how someone can use it to take his or her business to the next level. And then we had the idea to include the stories of other women who have also found the value of making authentic connections in their businesses.

It's been an extremely fascinating project, and it's taught me more than I could have ever imagined.

Wright

So the two of you interviewed these ladies and what did you find out?

Platske

The process was more comprehensive than interviewing a random sampling/group of women. First, Ursula and I created a list of the women we knew. Then we came up with the formula for what makes an *authentic connector.* And finally we asked ourselves, "Have we ever seen it in the women we know?"

Immediately, we answered with a resounding, "Yes!" After much deliberating and qualifying (as we each had to pitch the reasons why a particular woman should be in the book), Ursula and I sent an invitation to the women on our "final" list, inviting them to a special evening. The invitation was formal, similar to what you would receive for a wedding or cocktail reception, and the gathering was held at the local country club. We didn't tell them why they were invited or what the event was about because we wanted the women to truly want to be there more than anywhere else that night.

Our original list of invitees was twenty-two women. Obviously, some of them couldn't be there, but we set our intentions for fifteen people to attend, and that's exactly what we got!

When we unveiled our idea for the "legacy project," the response was incredible. The women were happy and eager to share their individual stories of how authentic connections helped their businesses grow.

Wright

In other words how they overcame obstacles, that sort of thing?

Platske

Well, our goal was to find out how they had used authentic connections to benefit their businesses, and some of their stories do include the obstacles they had to overcome. Others seem to have been born with a natural ability to form authentic connections. We found it truly remarkable that women from such diverse backgrounds had all discovered a "secret formula" for creating authentic connections and used it to take their businesses to the next level.

Wright

Lisa Marie, what advice would you impart to individuals who were looking to follow your secrets to success?

Platske

I believe that being an Upside Thinker is *the* secret to success. In fact, I believe this so passionately that I recently wrote a book titled *Designing Your Destiny: Achieving Personal and Professional Success through Upside Thinking* in order to help people become Upside Thinkers and transform their lives. It's meant to help them integrate my principles into their businesses and personal lives by guiding them through the process of analyzing their current state of excellence, discovering what they truly want for themselves, and then mapping a course to achieve it.

I believe there are five simple steps to creating an Upside Life:

> ➢ First, and I believe most important, is to have that written plan. If you're looking to succeed in business and your personal life, you need a clear vision with written goals—one in which you outline your mission and values to make sure you stay on course.

> ➢ The second step is discovering who your upside impact partners are. Who makes the biggest impact in your life right now? Who has the ability to add momentum and power to your achievement of those written goals? Then form those strategic business partnerships. If you're an Authentic Connector and sharer of information who comes from a place of abundance and views business as a way to serve others, then fame and fortune will follow. I'm a firm believer in this and a living example of its truth.

> ➢ The third step is setting your priorities—choosing to put your health and family before your work so you can be your absolute best in every pursuit.

> ➢ The fourth one is to live with an attitude of gratitude and enjoy the journey. Be grateful for every challenge and every opportunity that comes your way. Give thanks for every moment in order to be present to see the miracles around you and appreciate your friends, your family, and your colleagues for who they are, not who you want them to be. I keep a gratitude journal and take time out of my life every day to recognize all that is good in my life. I have found this to be a rewarding exercise that helps me to stay

in a place where the Law of Attraction works to my benefit.

> The fifth step to creating an Upside Life is the most difficult. It's choosing to be kind rather than choosing to be right. I think it goes back to, "Think before you speak." Think about whether what you're going to say is necessary or uplifting. If it's not, you shouldn't say it. This is so important in family and business relationships because when we focus on "getting points" for being right, we run the risk of losing relationships in the process.

In summary: create a written plan for your life; know who your impact partners are; set your priorities with your Self and Health first, Family second, and Work third; live with an attitude of gratitude, giving thanks for every challenge that comes your way; and choose to be kind rather than right.

Wright
That's heavyweight stuff. No wonder you're successful.

Platske
Yes, it is. It can revolutionize your life and enable you to enjoy your own personal journey of excellence.

Wright
This has been a great conversation. I really appreciate your taking all this time. Is there any parting advice you would like to give to our readers before we wrap it up?

Platske
Yes. I would like to encourage every reader to consider the possibility that they truly can design their own destiny by reflecting on their life as it is now, deciding what they really want, creating a plan to achieve it, and integrating the upside thinking principles to make it happen. If you need help, then find a coach to help you chart your course and hold you accountable to your goals. Finally, choose to "Ride the Upside"!

Wright

Lisa Marie, thank you so much for being with us today on *Speaking of Success.*

Platske

Thank you again for the opportunity.

About the Author

LISA MARIE PLATSKE, President and CEO of Upside Thinking, Inc., radiates a high-energy presence that immediately involves people and inspires them to create positive changes in their professional and personal lives.

Drawing on fifteen years of leadership experience in both the public and private sectors, she uses her background in banking and federal law enforcement and as an entrepreneur, author, and leadership coach to create unforgettable presentations and coaching sessions. Audiences and clients rave about her humor, powerful instruction, and relentless passion for helping people achieve more happiness, success, and meaning.

Lisa Marie's goal is to transform lives by helping others to see the possibilities, identify what they truly want professionally and personally, and use the three principles of Upside Thinking to achieve long-lasting results. Her approach is unique in that she empowers professionals to become happier, more balanced, and increasingly productive by focusing on integrating the whole person—mind, body, and spirit—as she helps them develop an authentic and clear leadership vision, increase their sphere of influence, and achieve long-term growth and steady profits. Lisa Marie's book, *Designing Your Destiny*, was written with this purpose in mind. She has also co-authored *Authentic Connections in Business* to help professionals unlock another secret to success in business and life.

In 2007, her vision, creativity, and service to others were recognized by the National Association of Female Executives that presented her with a Woman of Excellence award. She was recently featured in the *Press Enterprise, The Business Journal, The San Bernardino Sun,* and the *951* magazine.

Lisa Marie Platske
Upside Thinking, Inc.
5225 Canyon Crest Dr., Suite 71–154
Riverside, CA 92507
Phone: 951.334.9162
E-mail: leadershipstrategies@upsidethinking.com
www.upsidethinking.com

Chapter 11

HAZEL WAGNER

THE INTERVIEW

David Wright (Wright)

Hazel Wagner has an unusual and very eclectic background. She has a PhD in Mathematics and an MBA in International Marketing and Finance.

She succeeded as a technology salesperson, directed a worldwide marketing program, and built business relationships with international consulting organizations such as Deloitte and Touche and Ernst & Young.

When Hazel worked in the computer industry, she was continually promoted into increasing responsibility and larger scope.

When she retired the *first* time, as she likes to say, she started her own consulting firm, B9D, and recently started Brainiance Business Book Publishing which will be publishing the *Brainiance* series and producing seminars and workshops. During all those years she found opportunities to remain part of the academic world by teaching marketing at Kellogg Graduate School of Management and DePaul Graduate School of Business.

As a Course Leader for the American Management Association, Hazel delivers courses on leadership, marketing, strategy, critical thinking, and management. Currently she is writing a book, consulting, running her company, teaching, and providing seminars and workshops for businesses seeking to become more whole-brained.

Hazel, welcome to *Speaking of Success.*

Hazel Wagner (Wagner)
Thank you.

Wright
What is your definition of success?

Wagner
Being able to do the things you love, work with people who share your values, and earn a good living doing it. I love my father's definition: making at least one dollar more than you need. For me, doing the things I love means continuing to learn something new every day and share whatever I learn with at least two others who can benefit from it to multiply the effect. Of course, in my workshops and seminars I am able to share with many more than two at a time.

Business, like life in general, is all about people. So the ability to build mutually supportive relationships is crucial. For that to happen, there must be a set of shared values, often not actually discussed, but felt strongly—mutual trust, integrity, and loyalty.

Wright
Has your definition of success changed over time?

Wagner
Absolutely. First let's talk about business success, which is only a part of success in life.

When I was younger and working for large F100 companies, success was all about getting promoted—moving up in the company. I was focused on doing what I was assigned, meeting, and exceeding my quotas and goals. I focused on short-term goals.

Eventually I realized that to achieve true success and the rewards that come with it would require contribution at a much more important level—to the vision and direction of the organization. This requires a major effort to make a difference for the company in addition to handling the inevitable changes smoothly and building meaningful, productive working relationships with business associates both inside and outside the company. Again, I'm emphasizing the importance of people relationships.

Change has become something so prevalent and so constant that how people handle change is a sign of their potential and a requirement for success in any field.

I believe there are three requirements for success in the marketplace today:

1. The ability to collaborate—the ability to work well with people from every background and thinking style.
2. A continuous thirst for knowledge—the drive to learn from every situation you encounter, to learn as much as possible about business applicable subjects, and about the world at large.
3. The flexibility and adaptability to deal with change.

Companies need high-level business generalists—observant learners who can adapt to new tasks and can shift focus when needed. No matter what a person's role, it's the active awareness and understanding of that role and how it fits with the rest of the organization to make significant contributions to the organization as a whole that is important. This is the measure by which a person moves up the ladder, whether it's a corporate or an entrepreneurial ladder.

Wright

Since you talk about whole brain thinking and brainpower, and what you call "brainiance," are there elements that one must be born with and others that can be learned?

Wagner

We are born with the capacity and curiosity to learn. Just watch a young child explore his or her environment. Children look, listen, feel, taste, and sense other clues. The desire to learn is there. As people grow older they start tuning out "stuff" that they think they don't need. A more businesslike way to say it is that they learn how to focus.

Although screening out distractions is extremely important, we need to recognize that our personal thinking style, which differs in large or small ways from that of our co-workers, dictates how and to what we pay attention. It also determines what we may find annoying about how others approach the same situation.

The steps to Brainiance™, which means business (w)holistic thinking, are:

- Understand your own style (best done with one of the many instruments available such as MBTI®, HBDI®, DISC®, Extended DISC®, Mindex®).
- Recognize how others perceive the idiosyncrasies of your style.
- Learn the cues to recognize others' styles.
- Expand your own ability to "flex" with other styles both for understanding and to apply your personal Brainiance™.
- Help your organization become more Brainiant™ through organization-wide understanding, acceptance, and flexibility of thinking styles.

The Brainiance™ techniques of working on a team and collaborating result in much better decisions. People are perceived as decisive and the decisions are more successful.

Wright

What values and intellect are necessary for success?

Wagner

That is a very interesting question. I actually do a lot of work on values in some of my workshops and seminars. When I ask people what values they would miss most in coworkers, the two that come out at the top every time are integrity and trust. To be successful working with other people requires mutual integrity and trust; and each person's personal definitions have to be similar.

Examine what it means to be both trustworthy and to trust others. The mutuality is what builds a great working relationship. Build trusting productive teams and be known as a helpful collaborator, and your success is nearly assured.

Wright

What are the biggest obstacles to success for most people? What can get in the way of success?

Wagner

First, I would add to John Dunn's famous quote: "No man is an island" by saying, "No *company* is an island." We live in a world where collaboration, connection, and knowing what customers need is vital.

No company can succeed by isolating itself and no person inside a company can work successfully without collaboration. It is crucial to be viewed as someone who gets along with others, seeks out collaboration, and shares knowledge.

Second (and this may seem counter-intuitive), becoming an expert in one narrow skill area is not enough anymore. It's important to have areas in which you are considered an expert, but you also need to know how that area fits and fosters the overall success of your organization.

Companies need management and workers who are independent thinkers and generalists. People who have expertise in some critical areas of the business must also understand how that area fits into the larger picture and show interest in what is happening in the rest of the business and the world.

Finally, an individual has to possess and display energy, drive, and enthusiasm. Enthusiasm is extremely contagious. When you feel enthusiastic and you foster enthusiasm in colleagues, you work together better and productivity goes up.

People view others who have a lot of energy and drive as someone who will get ahead.

Wright

How did you end up in the field of sales and marketing in the technology industry after all those years in mathematics and academia?

Wagner

I loved teaching and realized I was good at simplifying complex subjects to achieve real understanding. Committing a subject to memory just long enough to pass a test is not real learning. True learning results when you understand the concepts well enough to apply them in different situations. This concept translates to business situations in which we must apply what we already know and understand how to produce innovative results.

In business we need to pool our ideas and share what we know. We need to ask each other really good questions—deep questions—using the Socratic Method. Instead of the typical test and school measures of success, in business we need to think that there are many right answers and to explore multiple possibilities. It is quite different from formal education, but my work in education led me into the world of business, which then led me to speaking and writing. I speak about differences in styles of learning, collaboration, and leadership, and how understanding these differences produces extraordinary results in business.

The number of changes in my career brought me through a full and fulfilling circle.

Wright

You seem to have led at least three lives, how did you do it all? And why do it all?

Wagner

When I look back I *have* been leading three lives. What connects those three lives is my basic motivation. I always needed to work and earn a living in ways that mattered, I needed to continue to feed my intense desire to learn and share that learning with others (what I call the ripple effect), and my family is where I am grounded.

I worked in education, then the computer technology industry. I worked in sales and marketing and several other areas of management, and eventually started my own consulting company, B9D (Beyond 9 Dots), Inc.

There was never a part I was willing to give up. Knowledge in diverse subjects gave me opportunities that wouldn't have happened any other way.

For example, a start-up company developing technology for schools brought me in as a long-term consultant because I understood technology, marketing, sales, schools, and the politics and decision-making of school districts.

The more diverse your areas of knowledge the more likely you will find a successful niche that few others can fill.

Wright

Did you or do you have any role models other than personal ones?

Wagner

I have several: Leonardo da Vinci and two living authors, Michael Gelb and Tony Buzan. Da Vinci because he pursued any path to which he felt drawn and was a genius in so many fields. Michael Gelb studied geniuses in history and has written great books so that we can all benefit from those histories. And Tony Buzan because he became interested in how our brain learns and remembers, and has been writing books for all ages and backgrounds on how to improve our learning and memory.

Da Vinci's interests in so many subjects led him to study other fields. His artwork led him to learn about anatomy, and then anatomy led him to medicine. Each field of interest contributed to his better understanding of the other fields. He was an absolutely amazing person. We know from documents found after he died that he kept journals of his ideas and thoughts and he often drew mind maps.

My second role model, Tony Buzan, writes books on the subject of mind mapping. I discovered mind mapping too late to help me while I was in school but I wish I had known about that study tool. The process of organizing a subject into a mind map forces understanding and works with nearly any subject and, therefore, improves memory. If only I had known about mind mapping I would not have had to suffer through so many all-night study sessions.

Mind mapping helps us use our brains much more effectively, or what I call (w)holistically. Brainiance™ is about using diversity of thinking styles and thinking improvement tools to help business professionals. Buzan has done a lot of work to understand how the brain works and his books teach us mind mapping.

My third role model is also a current author, Michael Gelb, who has written books about geniuses to help us learn how to bring out the inner genius in us. He wrote about Leonardo da Vinci and a number of others from history he deems geniuses.

Other than my family, these three men have had the most impact on the direction of my interests and work.

Wright

What inspired you to get into the speaking business?

Wagner

Speaking is a capstone for people who have done a lot of different things in their life and worked very hard to help other people learn. I always want to feel that everything I have learned I can share with a minimum of two other people so that I am creating a ripple effect with the knowledge and skills I share. It makes me feel that I am able to share more of what I have learned and help more people.

I can help others understand their own learning style and how to enhance it. When businesspeople recognize and appreciate the difference in styles of learning, working, and decision-making, they can apply it to collaboration, teams, and customers.

Teaching about what I have learned gives purpose to all the years I have spent, and continue to spend, studying more effective learning, differences in thinking and decision styles, marketing, sales, and even mathematics—all as they apply to making businesses and their employees more successful.

I want to empower businesses to be great places to work, attracting and keeping excellent employees, and inviting places for customers to do business. I provide businesses with the tools to accomplish that. I help companies inspire their employees to use Brainiance™ holistic thinking to raise the level of creativity and innovation.

The result is motivated employees and loyal customers, collaborative and productive teamwork.

Wright

What message would you want to send others to help them achieve success?

Wagner

The following is my list of what I want others to remember. These elements will help them reach success:

- Show how much drive you have (both biological and emotional), energy, passion, and persistence.
- See obstacles and mistakes as opportunities for learning.
- Keep up your education, either formal or self-taught.
- Encourage your curiosity.
- The most important trait for success is the ability to build great relationships by understanding everyone's differences in thinking styles. Practice this trait with your associates, customers, and others in your life.
- And finally, feel pride in doing a great job.

Wright

Today we have been speaking with Hazel Wagner. Hazel worked in the computer industry and was continually promoted into increasing responsibility and larger scope.

When she retired the *first* time, as she likes to say, she started her own consulting firm, B9D®. She recently started Brainiance Business Books™ Publishing, which will be publishing the *Brainiance* series and producing seminars and workshops. During all those years she found opportunities to stay part of the academic world including teaching marketing at Kellogg Graduate School of Management and DePaul Graduate School of Business.

As a Course Leader for the American Management Association, Hazel delivers courses on Leadership, Marketing, Strategy, Critical Thinking, and Management.

Currently she is writing a book, she consults, runs her company, teaches, and provides seminars and workshops for businesses seeking to become more whole-brained.

About the Author

DR. HAZEL WAGNER is an author, speaker, consultant, and entrepreneur. She has invested more than twenty-five years in technology, sales, and marketing and in educating businesspeople. She holds a PhD in mathematics and an MBA in International Marketing and Finance. She has worked and/or consulted for public and private corporations, Fortune 100s, start-ups, and for major universities. She is also an entrepreneur running her own consulting firm for more than fifteen years. In July 2000, she was named by *I-Street* magazine as one of the top twenty-five women in technology in the Chicago area.

Hazel Wagner, PhD
Speaker, Author, Consultant
B9D, Inc. Consulting
Brainiance Business Books
784 Sanday Lane
Barrington, IL 60010
Phone: 847.304.4999
E-mail: hazel.wagner@b9d.com
www.b9d.com
www.brainiance.com
www.hazelwagner.com

Photographs copyright
Wancket Studios
www.wancketstudios.com

Chapter 12

CHRISTY POTURKOVIC

THE INTERVIEW

David Wright (Wright)

Today we're talking with Christy Poturkovic. She is a Certified Empowerment Coach, speaker, and facilitator with more than twenty-five years of business and sales experience. Her diverse background includes sales, management, product evaluation, and long-range planning. She has worked with individuals and groups from the board room to the front lines to define desired results and achieve them.

Christy is passionate about helping people discover and achieve their full potential by building on their inherent strengths. She provides a proven process that enables clients to create a plan that will help them achieve a higher degree of success, both personally and professionally. Her approach helps her clients expand the attitudes, skills, knowledge, and habits that result in sustainable change.

Her guiding principle is: "It is better to dare mighty deeds than to live a life of quiet desperation and wonder what might have been."

Christy, you talk about attitude and how that affects our success. Tell us more about that.

Christy Poturkovic (Poturkovic)

We were all born with a tremendous amount of power and potential. What really drove that point home for me was my two-year-old granddaughter. She's just a little tiny girl, but nothing stops her. She thinks she can do whatever she wants or attempts to do. She watched the trapeze artists at the circus and said, "I swing too." I know she can't swing, but she doesn't know that. She looks at something and thinks, "Hey, I might like that, I think I'll give it a try." When most adults watch trapeze artists, they're thinking, "Where's the net? I hope they don't fall. I could never do that." As adults we're more often looking at what can go wrong and how we might fail. Kids don't naturally look at things and see the down side or the obstacles, they see the possibilities. Unfortunately, that ability starts getting chipped away as they grow.

Wright

What causes people to start shifting away from their natural optimism?

Poturkovic

Scientists tell us that the majority of our attitudes and beliefs are developed by the age of five and we carry these attitudes with us for the rest of our lives! Our attitudes, fears, and beliefs aren't something we're born with, they are learned. They are developed from our conditioning—the environment we grow up in, the input we receive from our parents and the other people in our lives. When we're little we don't have filters to make judgments for ourselves about what's right or wrong, we just accept whatever we're told.

Unfortunately, most of our conditioning is negative. That's not because our parents were trying to be mean to us, but because they are trying to protect us and shape our behavior. According to a UCLA study, a one-year-old child hears the word "no" more than 400 times per day. So by the time a child is four, he's been told "no" more than half a million times! The bottom line is that toddlers from all cultures and across all time lines learn what to do by constantly being told what not to do. This conditioning continues when we get to school— our teachers tell us don't talk in class, don't color outside the lines, etc. Eventually the don'ts of childhood become the can'ts of adulthood.

Wright

So how can that conditioning impact our success?

Poturkovic
Simply put, our conditioning results in our attitudes and our attitudes direct our behavior. Our behavior determines the results we get.

Here's the kicker: scientists estimate that about 88 percent of our behavior is habitual. Okay, we all know what habits are, but let's look at the *American Heritage Dictionary* definition: "A habit is a recurrent, often unconscious pattern of behavior that is acquired through frequent repetition." Simply put, a habit is a routine or behavior we keep repeating.

Notice the definition includes the word "*unconscious.*" Think of all the routines—and routines are habits—you follow every single day from the time you get up until the time you go to bed. How do you brush your teeth or drive to work? What about tying your shoes? What do you do as soon as you get to your office? Chances are you do most of these things the same way every day without even thinking about it. Having routines that we follow makes our lives easier—we don't have to think about each thing we're doing, evaluate it, try it, re-evaluate, and adjust. We've got it figured out so things flow pretty well.

But let's think about this for a minute: *almost 90 percent of our daily actions are performed unconsciously*, and it's our everyday actions that, for the most part, determine the results in our lives.

The problem is that when so much of what we do is on autopilot, we tend to become complacent and start settling for less than we're capable of.

I like to ask my clients how it would serve them better (and their family, their co-workers, and clients too) if they were *A Force To Be Reckoned With*? When I say that, some people may get a negative image, thinking it sounds a little negative, maybe too direct or pushy. But let's take a closer look. "Force" is defined as strength, energy, capability, power to influence. So *A Force To Be Reckoned With* is a powerful and influential person or thing. That's all good. The best part is we all have the ability to be *A Force To Be Reckoned With*; sometimes we just haven't realized it yet, or maybe we've forgotten how.

Wright
What are some steps you can take to help you get started in reclaiming your own personal power?

Poturkovic

It all starts with your thoughts, the way you talk to yourself, or what might even be sometimes called "head trash." Researchers tell us that we have approximately sixty thousand thoughts per day. They also tell us that about 83 percent of our thought patterns are negative. That's more than 49,000 negative thoughts in one day! Most people will say, "No way, I'm a positive person," but just pay attention to your thoughts sometime. I'll bet that when someone does something you don't like, maybe cuts you off in traffic, you spend some time thinking, "What a jerk." Perhaps when you're asked to do something new or outside your comfort zone your first thought might be, "I can't do that." When you don't get the results you want you may be thinking, "Why did I do that?" or "I'm such an idiot" or "I know they won't return my call." Unfortunately, because we're so used to it, we're not even aware most of the time of the negative thought stream going on in our heads. In fact, those negative thoughts are habits, and like any habit they can be changed.

Wright

Once we're aware of our habits of thought, what can we do to change them?

Poturkovic

The best way to change your attitude is to change your input. I'm sure you're familiar with the old computer industry saying: "garbage in, garbage out." The same is true with people.

One easy way to change your input is to cut back on the amount of time spent watching television. If you spend one hour per day watching television, it equates to just over fifteen full twenty-four-hour days per year spent watching television. That's more than a two-week vacation. Another way to look at it is *forty-five* eight-hour work days—that's nine workweeks! Will watching the evening news, *American Idol*, or *The Office* help you achieve your goals? What else could you do with that time that would be stimulating, enriching, or enjoyable? What could you do instead that would help you achieve the things you desire in life?

Another way to start changing your attitudes is to be aware of the way you talk to yourself. Okay, this could be getting a little too touchy-feely, but bear with me. What does the voice in your head consistently say to you? Does it say, "Don't try that, you might fail?" "I'm always late?" "I'm disorganized?"

Think about this (I'm just imagining here, but I'll bet I'm not far off): Remember the Super Bowl and all the talk about Peyton Manning getting the monkey off his back? Do you think he went in to that game thinking, "I hope I don't fail?" or "I hope I don't mess up? People say I choke, and can't handle a clutch situation. I hope I don't throw any interceptions." I don't think so. I'm sure he focused on what he does do well and filled his mind with thoughts about doing it well. How can you apply that same approach in your life?

Affirmations are another way to shift attitudes that works for many people. Affirmations are positive statements regarding your goals. They should be realistically high, but believable, and should be repeated at least three times a day. Post them someplace where you'll see them frequently. Affirmations, like the other approaches I've mentioned, work because whatever we permit to enter and remain in our minds will eventually reveal itself in our behavior and in our success or failure.

Another great technique that I really like is visualization, and the clearer you can visualize, the better. This was a lesson I learned as a child. I wanted to learn how to do a back handspring; it was a big deal for me, but I hadn't mastered it yet. I practiced endlessly but couldn't do it by myself. My dad told me to visualize myself doing it, and to actually feel what it would feel like. I can remember lying in bed doing just that, and it wasn't long until I could do a really good back handspring.

Another visualization technique that I like is to use pictures. I have compiled an assortment of pictures that represent places I want to go, goals I want to achieve, things I want to own, etc. I keep it handy and look through it periodically like a catalog.

Regardless of whether it's a skill you're trying to master, something tangible you want, or the outcome of a meeting, when you visualize clearly the outcome you want you're involving your subconscious mind, which will set to work giving you your desired outcome. When you're focused on your desired outcome—as opposed to what you don't want to happen—chances are very high that you will perform better. Remember, what you focus on the most is what you get more of! Your mind is constantly working to turn your thinking into reality. It's really important to take conscious control over your thought processes. If you don't, you're at the mercy of your environment and that's not necessarily the best place to be!

Wright

You mentioned habits of thought, what other habits are important to success?

Poturkovic

The most important habit for success is confidence. Most people think of confidence as something they either have or they don't. But confidence is nothing more than a habit that can be honed. I learned that lesson early in my career. I had just turned twenty-one and was working in what was at the time a new industry—telecommunications. Most of the people I worked with were at least fifteen years older than I was and I was concerned that I wouldn't be taken seriously because of my age. I remember talking with my dad about it and he told me, "Act confident, be confident"—the old "fake it till you make it" routine; but it works. That was probably some of the best advice I ever got.

Wright

What can you do to act confident?

Poturkovic

When you think of people who appear very confident, what do you notice about them? It's usually the way they look, the way they speak, their energy, enthusiasm, and their knowledge. Obviously we need to pay attention to our appearance and gain the knowledge and experience we need, but one of the simplest and most powerful ways to start projecting more confidence immediately is with the words we choose.

Just like the clothes we wear, the words we choose can have a powerful impact on how others perceive us. To immediately appear and feel more confident, be aware of how you speak.

Avoid using tentative words such as "probably," "maybe," "I think so," "I'd like to." They make you sound weak. Instead use action words that accurately describe what you'll do. Instead of "I think so," state what you know. Instead of "I'll try," state what you'll do. Just like Yoda said in *Star Wars Episode V,* "Try not. Do . . . or do not. There is no try."

Avoid the word "hopefully." No one pays you for what you'll hopefully get done. Instead state what you *will* do.

Another phrase that has crept into many people's daily conversations is "I'm sorry" when they're expressing an opinion. For example, "I'm sorry, I like Coke better than Pepsi" or "I'm sorry, I disagree with that policy." Why are you sorry? "I'm sorry" is a state of being. Unless you're truly making an apology, using the word "sorry" invalidates what you're saying. And if you are making an apology, say, "I apologize," rather than, "I'm sorry;" then offer a solution to remedy the situation.

So stop using tentative words and use power words instead. Power words are strong words that capture your listener's attention. There are many power words and a few examples are: absolutely, guaranteed, unbelievable, ultimate, and powerful.

Obviously you wouldn't want to use them all in one sentence! As a simple example, which statement would intrigue a listener more: "I've got great news" or "I've got fantastic news"?

If you sprinkle your conversation with power words you are guaranteed to garner more attention from your listeners.

Wright

I understand how important attitude is, but what else?

Poturkovic

You're right—a success attitude is only part of the equation. The right attitude is the critical starting point, but without action, nothing happens. The good news is, by developing a success attitude you will naturally propel yourself into action. A clear vision provides your direction. What do you really want to accomplish, to have, and to be? The more clearly focused you are, the more satisfaction you'll get from your results.

I think the reason most people don't achieve the results they want is they don't take the first fundamental step that's required once they decide what it is they want to achieve. They may state what they want, they may even write it down, but that's where it stops. In order to achieve the results you want, you have to have a written plan. Think about this: Most of the time when we go to the grocery store we make a list. Why? We don't want to forget anything and waste our time going back. How much more important is it then to have a written plan for our lives? You need to be clear about what you want to accomplish, when you want to accomplish it, and what you're going to do to make it happen. Writing it down gives it more permanence than just stating or thinking about it. Writing also provides more focus and clarity.

Vision and planning are the starting point. As the Japanese proverb says, "Vision without action is a daydream. Action without vision is a nightmare!"

Wright

How do you coach someone through an effective planning process?

Poturkovic

The planning process involves identifying the actions that will need to be taken to achieve your vision. So the first step is to clearly state your vision in writing. Once the vision is clear, I encourage people to look into their motivation for achieving their goal. There are two basic reasons we have for setting goals—we want the reward of achieving it or we want to avoid the consequences of not achieving it.

I ask my clients why that goal is important to them, what will it mean to them to achieve it? I try to get their senses and emotions involved. What will it look like, how will you feel? What will you hear? The more emotional connection there is to a goal, the more your brain will kick in to make it happen. It's important to dig into that deeply and uncover the bigger rewards, which are not usually the first reasons given. Then we discuss the consequences of not achieving the goal, again bringing all the senses and emotions into play. The purpose of that process is to emotionalize the goal, which provides the motivation to do what it will take to achieve it.

Next we uncover all the obstacles that might stand in their way. It's really a brainstorming session. We want to identify all the possible stumbling blocks—anything that can possibly prevent them from achieving their goal. After all the obstacles have been identified, we brainstorm all the possible solutions for overcoming them. Since it's brainstorming, we write everything down. After we've identified every possible solution, we identify specific actions that can be taken to implement those solutions, assign target dates to begin and complete those actions, and determine if they can be delegated and to whom.

Delegation is often a difficult topic. Frequently the first thought is, "No, I have to do it. I can't delegate this." When we start talking about delegating, I encourage my clients to consider what they do exceptionally well. We're all blessed with a variety of talents and abilities. We're pretty good at some things, excellent at others, and there are some things that are probably best to avoid. For example, accounting and bookkeeping are areas for me that I should stay away from! If I invest a lot of my time in those areas, I end up frustrated. It also keeps me from spending my time on activities that will produce the results I want. I could take an accounting class, but that's not going to maximize my strengths, so the best thing for me to do is find someone else to handle my bookkeeping for me.

Unfortunately most of us grew up being taught to improve upon our weaknesses rather than building upon our strengths. The rationale was that we'd have a broad level of competency. But the reality is that by focusing on our weaknesses we usually just end up with stronger weaknesses! The only way to really excel is to maximize your strengths. How can you spend more of your time and energy doing what you're truly brilliant at? I don't mean you should ignore your weaknesses, but find a way to manage them so that you can more clearly focus on doing what you do best. A good rule of thumb is, if you don't like to do it, delegate it—as often as possible!

So planning is critical. Very rarely do people achieve the income they want or the position they want or really anything they want by *hoping* they will. Of course we all have hopes, but our hopes have to be backed up by a specific plan of action with daily follow-up. Hope is not a strategy! Why would you want to go about your business or your life just *hoping* things will work out for you? Hoping is rather disempowering; but when you have a specific plan and act on it every day, the outcome is up to you.

Wright

Many people make great plans, but they seem to stop at the planning process. What are some keys to executing our plans?

Poturkovic

Often, the focus and planning part is easy; that's where the excitement is—laying it all out and seeing the possibilities. But for many people, execution is the hard part. We may know all the right things to do, we may really want to do them, but something holds us back. What is it?

Our attitudes—those "habits of thought" I mentioned earlier—hold us back. Without being aware they're doing it, people often think more about what's going to go wrong—how they are going to fail—than what could go right and how they will succeed. That negative thought process, which generates fear within us, is what most often keeps us from taking action.

I often ask my clients what attitudes they have that are holding them back. I ask them to get out a blank piece of paper and at the top write, "What's Holding Me Back?" Then take no more than five uninterrupted minutes and list everything that comes to mind. Don't censor or judge it, just write everything down. When they're done, I ask them to put the list away for twenty-four hours, then get it back out and start putting together a plan to address each item. The good news is, you can change your attitude, but it must be a conscious effort. Just recognizing your habits of thought is the first step to changing them, and having a winning attitude is critical to your success.

So if you really want to take action, you're motivated, you're determined to achieve your goals, and you're trying to change your attitudes, what can you do when resistance sets in? One approach is to just dive right in and go for it. I like to use the analogy of jumping into a cold swimming pool. It's really uncomfortable at first but the more you thrash around, the more comfortable you become. For other people, a slow, steady approach works best. Either way, when embarking on a path of change, it's helpful to have an "accountability partner"—a friend or colleague or better yet, a coach—who is committed to helping you stay on track with your goal. Whatever approach works best for you is fine, but if you're committed to reaching the success you desire, you're going to have to take action. Nike has been telling us for years to: "Just Do It." I say: "Just Do It Now!"

About the Author

CHRISTY POTURKOVIC is a Certified Empowerment Coach, speaker, and facilitator with more than twenty-five years of business and sales experience. Her diverse background includes sales, management, product evaluation, and long-range planning. She has worked with individuals and groups from the boardroom to the front lines to define desired results and achieve them.

Christy is passionate about helping people discover and achieve their full potential by building on their inherent strengths. She provides a proven process that enables clients to create a plan that will help them achieve a higher degree of success, both personally and professionally. Her approach helps her clients expand the attitudes, skills, knowledge, and habits that result in sustainable change.

Her guiding principle is: "It is better to dare mighty deeds than to live a life of quiet desperation and wonder what might have been."

Christy Poturkovic
P.O. Box 342
Fishers, IN
Phone: 317.845.5017
E-mail: ChristyP@SuccessStrategiesLLC.com
www.SuccessStrategiesLLC.com